W9-AEJ-567

An Introduction to the
SPECIAL THEORY
OF RELATIVITY

ROBERT KATZ, 1917-

Professor of Physics
Kansas State University

An Introduction to the
SPECIAL THEORY
OF RELATIVITY

Published for
The Commission on College Physics

BRIAR CLIFF COLLEGE
LIBRARY
SIOUX CITY, IOWA

D. VAN NOSTRAND COMPANY, INC.

Princeton, New Jersey

Toronto   London   New York

FOR STEVE AND JOHN

D. VAN NOSTRAND COMPANY, INC.
120 Alexander St., Princeton, New Jersey
(*Principal Office*)
24 West 40 Street, New York 18, New York

D. VAN NOSTRAND COMPANY, LTD.
358, Kensington High Street, London, W.14, England

D. VAN NOSTRAND COMPANY (Canada), LTD.
25 Hollinger Road, Toronto 16, Canada

COPYRIGHT © 1964, BY
D. VAN NOSTRAND COMPANY, INC.

Published simultaneously in Canada by
D. VAN NOSTRAND COMPANY (Canada), LTD.

*No reproduction in any form of this book, in
whole or in part (except for brief quotation in
critical articles or reviews), may be made without written authorization from the publishers*

QC
6
.R34

PRINTED IN THE UNITED STATES OF AMERICA

Preface

It is the purpose of this book to provide an introduction to the Special Theory of Relativity which is accessible to any student who has had an introduction to general physics and some slight acquaintance with the calculus. Much of the material is at a level suitable for high school students who have had advanced placement in physics and mathematics. Since some of the exposition, particularly part of Chapter 6, is presented here in book form for the first time, even terminal graduate students in physics may find the material profitable.

The subject matter of the book has been taught, in the form presented here, to first-year graduate students at Kansas State University for many years. Much of it has sifted into courses at lower level.

The typescript was read by Professors E. U. Condon, University of Colorado, and Melba Phillips, University of Chicago. I wish to thank them for their helpful criticism and valuable suggestions.

May 26, 1964
Manhattan, Kansas

ROBERT KATZ

50295

Table of Contents

1   *The Galilean Transformation*

§1-1 **The Inertial Frame** Does the earth move around the sun or the sun around the earth? Do we describe the motion of the moon by saying that it traces a nearly circular path around the earth, or a somewhat more complicated path around the sun? These questions are associated with the choice of a frame of reference, a background against which we imagine motions to be referred. The choice is not a simple one, since it has philosophic as well as physical overtones. The central position accorded to man in the universe led to the belief that the sun and stars circulate about the earth, and in consequence, the universe of Ptolemy (A.D. 127-151) demanded that heavenly bodies move in paths compounded from circles, called epicycles. The path of a point which moves on a small circle, whose center in turn moves on a larger circle, is called an epicycle. In part the composition of the paths of heavenly bodies from circles arose from the view that only the most perfect figure, the circle, was appropriate to any object in the heavens. Copernicus' (1473-1543) relocation of the origin of the coordinate frame to the sun led to a new grouping of the earth and planets as a system of solar satellites and resulted in a new set of physical laws, whose truth was universal, valid on earth and in heaven. These were the laws of Newton (1642-1727).

The philosophic implications of the relocation of the origin of astronomical coordinates have been widely elaborated under names like rationalism, or naturalism, or secularism. It is our purpose here to emphasize the importance of the choice of a coordinate frame in physics, though clearly the choice has far broader implications in the affairs of men.

The logical choice of a coordinate frame to Newton was one in which the stars were at rest. There are some physicists today to whom this choice seems a proper one. A concept called *Mach's Principle,* propounded by Ernst Mach (1838-1916), states that inertia is entirely due to the mutual action of matter, so that force is required to accelerate matter only because it is displaced relative to the other matter of the universe. More generally, physicists place a weaker restriction on the choice of a coordinate frame: the frame must be inertial. *An inertial frame is one in which Newton's first law is true.*

For many centuries before Newton, inquiries into the way the world was structured led to the belief that the natural state of things on earth was a state of rest—objects left alone remained at rest. To set them in motion and to keep them in motion was thought to require the application of a force. Newton's formulation gave equal importance to rest and to uniform motion in a straight line, and asserted that either of these states was natural; that is, either of these conditions would continue indefinitely if no force was applied. This was in great contradiction to earlier beliefs which supposed that force was required to sustain motion as well as to initiate motion.

Newton's First Law states: A body at rest remains at rest, and a body in motion will continue in motion with steady speed in a straight line as long as no outside force acts on the body.

Today we accept the first law as axiomatic, and use it as a recipe for finding a coordinate frame in which to describe physical systems. Unless otherwise stated all physical laws stated in this book (and in most others) are with respect to an inertial frame. The symbols which appear in physical equations represent quantities which are usually measured by observers stationed in an inertial frame.

A test for an inertial frame is simplicity itself. A frame of reference may be thought of as a mesh of lines. In free space, in the absence of gravitational or other force fields, a particle set down in an inertial frame may always be found there. If the particle is set in motion, it will move with steady speed in a straight line. Its coordinates, measured in this frame, will satisfy the equation of a straight line, and its motion along this line will be with constant speed. If the particle does not remain at the point at which it is placed, or does not move in a straight line with steady speed, then the frame is not inertial. A perfectly smooth, level, spinning turntable on earth is not an inertial frame. A particle placed on this turntable will remain at a single point with respect to the earth as the turntable slips under it, but it will describe a circular path with respect to the turntable. Thus the turntable is not an inertial frame, for though no forces act on the particle it is neither at rest nor moving in a straight line with constant speed with respect to the turntable.

Experiment has shown that Newton's frame of reference, fixed in the stars, is an inertial frame. A coordinate frame fixed in the earth is not inertial, due to the earth's rotation about its axis, and about the sun as well. For most practical purposes, and to the accuracy with which many experiments are performed, the fact that a frame fixed in the earth is not inertial does not alter the outcome of experiments sufficiently to cause concern. In fact it was only through the *Foucault pendulum* that the rotation of the earth was first clearly demonstrated, in 1851. Foucault (1819-1868) suspended a heavy pendulum bob by a long flexible wire, and observed that the plane of vibration of the pendulum rotated with respect to the floor. But there was no way the support point could twist the plane in which the pendulum oscillated once it had been started. He concluded that the floor was rotating beneath the pendulum. We infer from such an experiment that the earth is not an inertial frame. There are everyday experiences in which the distinction between inertial and non-inertial frames must be made. One of these lies in the circulation of the atmosphere, and another in the meaning of the term *centrifugal force*.

§1-2 **The Galilean Transformation**   Through his studies of projectile motion, Galileo (1564-1642) concluded that the motion of a projectile launched from the ground at an arbitrary angle could be derived from the motion of a projectile launched straight up. A projectile thrown straight up from a uniformly moving cart would be seen from the cart as moving straight up and down, but the motion seen from the ground could be predicted by superimposing the motion of the cart onto that of the projectile. These ideas of Galileo are the basis of the *Galilean transformation,* through which we relate motions as they are observed in two different inertial frames. We will see that Galilean transformations must be superseded by a different transformation, the Lorentz transformation, when the two frames move at great speeds with respect to each other. But for ordinary experience the Galilean transformation is much simpler and is quite satisfactory.

Let us suppose that two sets of observers are available to study a problem. One set is at rest with respect to the ground, and makes its measurements with respect to a coordinate frame and a set of clocks fixed in the ground and synchronized to read alike. We call the set of observers and the observations they make the *unprimed set,* and refer to their measured coordinates and time as $x, y, z, t,$ without primed superscripts. A second set of observers is at rest with respect to a second coordinate frame, the primed frame, which moves with constant velocity with respect to the unprimed frame, as if the second set of observers were riding on a large space platform. We will call the primed observers and their observations the *primed set.* We will refer to their observations as x', y', z', t'.

We choose the two sets of coordinates to be parallel. The x' axis is parallel to the x axis, the y' axis to the y axis, the z' axis parallel to the z axis. Further, we choose the orientation of the axes such that the motion of the primed frame is parallel to the x axis. The primed frame moves in the $+x$ direction with velocity V with respect to the unprimed frame. For convenience we choose the origins of the two sets of coordinates to coincide at times $t = t' = 0$, as in Fig. 1-2.1.

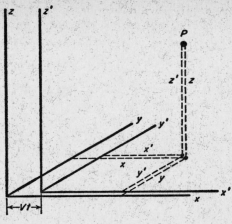

FIG. 1-2.1

Suppose that a particle is located at a point P at a particular time, and that measurements of the coordinates and the time are made by the two sets of observers. The measured values can be related by the equations

$$x' = x - Vt, \tag{1-2.1a}$$

$$y' = y, \tag{1-2.1b}$$

$$z' = z, \tag{1-2.1c}$$

and

$$t' = t. \tag{1-2.1d}$$

The equations 1-2.1 are the *Galilean transformation* equations, which relate the observations of position and time made by two sets of observers located on two different inertial frames, as described.

The point P may be on the path of a projectile. To describe the motion properly we need to say something about the velocity and the acceleration of the projectile. This implies that we wish to study differential increments of the coordinates in the two frames. We take differentials of the transformation equations 1-2.1, recalling that V is constant, to find

$$dx' = dx - V\,dt, \qquad (1\text{-}2.2\text{a})$$

$$dy' = dy, \qquad (1\text{-}2.2\text{b})$$

$$dz' = dz, \qquad (1\text{-}2.2\text{c})$$

and
$$dt' = dt. \qquad (1\text{-}2.2\text{d})$$

Now we divide each of the equations 1-2.2a-c by Eq. 1-2.2d to find transformation equations for the components of the velocity. We have

$$\frac{dx'}{dt'} = \frac{dx}{dt} - V, \quad \text{or} \quad v_{x'} = v_x - V. \qquad (1\text{-}2.3\text{a})$$

$$\frac{dy'}{dt'} = \frac{dy}{dt}, \qquad \text{or} \quad v_{y'} = v_y. \qquad (1\text{-}2.3\text{b})$$

$$\frac{dz'}{dt'} = \frac{dz}{dt}, \qquad \text{or} \quad v_{z'} = v_z. \qquad (1\text{-}2.3\text{c})$$

These results may be put into vector form by multiplying each of these equations by the appropriate unit vectors. A *unit vector* is a dimensionless quantity which indicates direction. Thus the unit vector $\mathbf{1}_x$ is parallel to the x axis and of magnitude 1. Our primed and unprimed coordinate axes are parallel so that $\mathbf{1}_{x'} = \mathbf{1}_x$, and so on. Thus if we multiply Eq. 1-2.3a by $\mathbf{1}_x$, Eq. 1-2.3b by $\mathbf{1}_y$, and Eq. 1-2.3c by $\mathbf{1}_z$ and add these equations, we find that

$$v_{x'}\mathbf{1}_{x'} + v_{y'}\mathbf{1}_{y'} + v_{z'}\mathbf{1}_{z'} = v_x\mathbf{1}_x + v_y\mathbf{1}_y + v_z\mathbf{1}_z - V\mathbf{1}_x,$$

which may be condensed to read

$$\mathbf{v}' = \mathbf{v} - \mathbf{V}. \qquad (1\text{-}2.4)$$

If we transpose the velocity of the primed frame with respect to the unprimed frame, we obtain

$$\mathbf{v} = \mathbf{v}' + \mathbf{V}. \qquad (1\text{-}2.5)$$

It is through Eq. 1-2.5 that the airspeed of an airplane is converted to groundspeed, using knowledge of the velocity of the air with respect to the ground. When we speak of windspeed we generally mean the speed an air mass is moving with respect to the ground. When we speak of the airspeed of an airplane, or its cruising speed, we mean the speed with which the airplane moves with respect to the air mass. For navigation with respect to the earth the groundspeed is required, or more precisely, the velocity with respect to the ground is required. The Galilean transformation makes air navigation possible.

In ordinary conversation we are sometimes careless about specifying the frame to which a position or a motion is referred. When we give the cruising speed of an airplane we may be vague in noting that it is with respect to the air mass through which the plane is moving. When we give the windspeed we may be vague in noting that this is with respect to the ground. Consider the question, with what speed is the air blowing past the wings of an airplane whose cruising speed is 200 miles per hour (mph) when it flies into a 50 mph headwind? By the definition of cruising speed the answer is 200 mph, when the airplane is operating properly. If the unprimed coordinate frame is fixed in the ground and the primed set is fixed in the air mass, then the design of the airplane implies that its speed v' is 200 mph for proper operation. If v' is very much less than 200 mph, the airplane falls down; if v' is much greater than 200 mph, the wings fall off.

Neither the magnitude of the velocity nor the direction of the path (the direction of the velocity vector) is the same in the two frames. As a simple illustration consider the motion of a boat on a river. Suppose that the water moves east at 3 mph and that a boat heads north at 4 mph with respect to the water (see Fig. 1-2.2). If we take east as the positive x direction and north as the positive y direction, then the motion of the boat with respect to the primed frame (fixed in the water) is

$$\mathbf{v}' = 4 \text{ mph} \times \mathbf{1}_{y'}.$$

Its motion with respect to the ground is the vector sum of the motion of the boat with respect to the water, $\mathbf{v}'$, and the motion of the water with respect to the ground, $\mathbf{V}$ (= 3 mph $\times$ $\mathbf{1}_x$). According to Eq. 1-2.5, we have

$$\mathbf{v} = (3 \, \mathbf{1}_x + 4 \, \mathbf{1}_y) \text{ mph}.$$

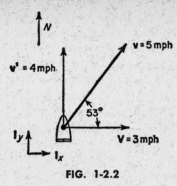

FIG. 1-2.2

The boat moves at 5 mph with respect to the ground in a direction 53° north of east.

To examine the way in which accelerations transform in two inertial frames, we may simply take time derivatives of Eq. 1-2.5, bearing in mind that $t = t'$. Thus we may differentiate $\mathbf{v}'$ with respect to t' and $\mathbf{v}$ with respect to t. Noting that $\mathbf{V}$ is constant, we find

$$\frac{d\mathbf{v}'}{dt'} = \frac{d\mathbf{v}}{dt},$$

or $\qquad\qquad\qquad \mathbf{a}' = \mathbf{a}.$ (1-2.6)

In this section we have been careful to emphasize that the time measured in both primed and unprimed frames has the same value, that the operation of clocks does not appear to depend on the speed with which they move. This view derives from ordinary experience which is summarized in the Galilean transformation equations. We have done this in anticipation of our study of relativity where a distinction must be made between measurements of time in two inertial frames. This distinction is one of the key problems of the special theory of relativity. While the Galilean transformation is extremely useful in the analysis of physical systems, the work of Lorentz and Einstein at the beginning of the present century showed it to be inadequate to describe the behavior of physical systems when the translational velocity

V is very large, of the order of the speed of light in vacuum (186,000 miles per second). When speeds approach the speed of light, physicists have learned that they must use a different set of transformation equations to relate motions in two inertial frames. These are called the Lorentz transformation equations. We will devote a great deal of attention to examining these equations and their consequences.

Nevertheless, although the Galilean transformation is now known to be inadequate to relate observations made on systems moving at high speeds to observations of the same systems moving slowly, it is simpler and sufficiently accurate in the limit of low velocities to be of great practical importance. Man has not yet learned to move anything but elementary particles and perhaps the nuclei of atoms at speeds approaching that of light. Thus for most practical purposes and for virtually all of engineering the Galilean transformation yields sufficiently correct results.

1-2.1 A ship heads due north at 30 mph with respect to the sea. A wind blows to the east at 40 mph with respect to the sea. Find the velocity of the wind with respect to the ship, as it might be measured by an observer on the ship. [50 mph, 37° south of east]

1-2.2 After going a mile upstream in a motor boat, a man accidentally drops an oar overboard. He proceeds upstream for 10 minutes before he misses the oar. He then turns round and retrieves the oar at the point from which he started originally. If the boat travels at constant speed with respect to the water, what is the speed of the current? Work the problem twice, in the frame fixed in the banks, and in the frame fixed in the stream. [3 mph]

1-2.3 A boy throws a stone to the east at 30 ft/sec from a northbound train traveling at 88 ft/sec on straight tracks. The stone's initial velocity is at 37° above the horizontal. The stone leaves the boy's hand at 10 ft above the ground. Find the parametric equations of motion of the stone with the point of projection as origin in a frame fixed in the ground, and in a frame fixed in the train.

§1-3 The Speed of Light In principle, measurement of the speed of light is not different from the measurement of any other speed. One measures the time required for light to travel over a measured path. The difficulty arises from its great rapidity, so that either long paths or short time intervals must be measured.

The first measurement of the speed of light was astronomical. In 1675 Olaf Roemer (1644-1710), a Danish astronomer, observed that a greater time elapsed between the eclipses of one of Jupiter's moons during the season the earth is receding from Jupiter, position E_1 in Fig. 1-3.1, than during the season the

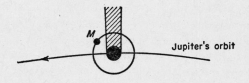

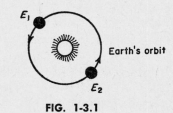

FIG. 1-3.1

earth is approaching Jupiter, position E_2 in Fig. 1-3.1. He interpreted this discrepancy as due to the finite speed of light, asserting that the light had to travel a greater distance between eclipses when the earth was receding than when the earth was approaching Jupiter. Roemer concluded that it took light 22 minutes to cross the earth's orbit, a distance of about 3×10^8 km, giving a speed of about 2.3×10^8 m/sec. Roemer's was a beautiful inference, giving a value within about 25 percent of the presently accepted value of the speed of light c, for today we take

$$c = 2.997925 \pm 0.000003 \times 10^8 \text{ m/sec.}$$

An earlier attempt to measure the speed of light was made by

Galileo, who stationed two observers with lanterns a mile apart. They were to signal each other by uncovering their lanterns according to a prearranged schedule. While such a system might have yielded a value for the speed of sound, it was unable to respond with sufficient speed to determine the speed of light. Subsequent experimenters replaced one of Galileo's observers with a mirror and replaced his crude measurement of time by the rotation of a toothed wheel. The toothed wheel was at once a shutter to let light pass and a clock, for, at the proper speed of rotation, light passing through one opening could reach the mirror and return through the next opening in the wheel. Such an arrangement was used much later by Fizeau (1819-1896) in 1849, with a base line of 8.633 km from source to mirror. In Fizeau's experiment the wheel had 720 teeth and rotated at 12.6 revolutions/sec. More modern experiments form a pulse of light (or other electromagnetic radiation) electronically, and detect it in a similar way. Today it is possible to measure time intervals nanoseconds (10^{-9}) long. But in principle the experimental measurement of the speed of light is closely related to the system used by Galileo.

Toward the end of the nineteenth century, as measurements of the speed of light became more refined, the question arose—What was the coordinate frame with respect to which the speed of light was measured? Was the speed of light which was measured its speed with respect to the earth? to the stars? to Jupiter? Was there a preferred medium for light, as air is a preferred medium for sound?

It is clear that sound travels through air, and that the speed of sound must be measured with respect to the air. Experiment shows that the velocity of sound with respect to the earth can be obtained by a Galilean transformation by adding the velocity of sound with respect to the air to the velocity of the air with respect to the earth. By analogy, physicists supposed that there was a preferred medium for light which filled infinite space. This medium was called the *ether*. The ether was thought to be perfectly transparent to light, and to offer no resistance to the passage of stars or the planets. Its function was to provide a coordinate frame to answer the question—"With respect to what is the velocity of light c?" Since the speed of the earth's orbital motion is about 30,000 m/sec, it was supposed that sensitive experiments might be devised to show that the speed of light with respect to the earth would depend on the direction the light traveled with respect to the earth's motion through the ether, in accordance to the Galilean transformation.

Consider an experimental apparatus which might be devised to study variations in the speed of light with respect to the earth, as related to the motion of the earth through space. Such an apparatus might compare the time for a light ray to pass down a rod and be reflected back, when the rod was parallel to the earth's motion, and then when the rod was perpendicular to the earth's motion.

Imagine an equipment consisting of a rod of length L provided with a mirror at one end, and with a pulsed light source, a detector, and a clock at the other end. In Fizeau's experiment the detector was the eye, and the light pulser-clock was the toothed wheel. With this idealized equipment, suitably scaled and suitably fast, we might measure the speed of light.

When the rod is *at rest* with respect to the ether, the time for the light to make a round trip is Δt_0, where

$$\Delta t_0 = 2L/c. \qquad (1\text{-}3.1\text{a})$$

When the rod is *moving* through the ether with speed v and is oriented *parallel* to its direction of motion, as in Fig. 1-3.2a, we find the speed of light with respect to the rod by the Galilean transformation, for this is the hypothesis to be tested. Then the speed of light with respect to the rod is $c - v$ when light is moving to the mirror, and $c + v$ on the return trip. The elapsed time for this trip is $\Delta t_{||}$, as given by

$$\Delta t_{||} = L/(c - v) + L/(c + v),$$

or
$$\Delta t_{||} = \frac{2L}{c} \frac{1}{(1 - v^2/c^2)}. \qquad (1\text{-}3.1\text{b})$$

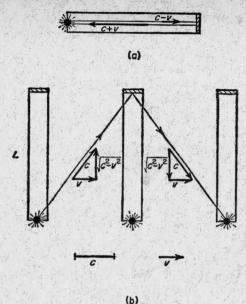

(a)

(b)

FIG. 1-3.2

Suppose the rod is moving through the ether with speed v, Fig. 1-3.2b, the rod being oriented perpendicular to its direction of motion. By the Galilean transformation the speed of light with respect to the rod is $(c^2 - v^2)^{1/2}$ on both the outgoing and the return trip, so that the elapsed time is $\Delta t_\perp$, given by

$$\Delta t_\perp = \frac{2L}{c} \frac{1}{(1 - v^2/c^2)^{1/2}}. \qquad (1\text{-}3.1c)$$

If we now make use of the binomial theorem for $(1 + x)^m$,

$$(1 + x)^m = 1 + \frac{mx}{1!} + \frac{m(m - 1)}{2!} x^2$$

$$+ \ldots \frac{m(m - 1) \ldots (m - n + 2)}{(n - 1)!} x^{n-1}, \qquad (1\text{-}3.2)$$

we may expand Eqs. 1-3.1b and c to the quadratic term to find

$$\Delta t_{\parallel} = \Delta t_0 (1 + v^2/c^2 + \ldots) \tag{1-3.3a}$$

and
$$\Delta t_{\perp} = \Delta t_0 (1 + \tfrac{1}{2} v^2/c^2 + \ldots). \tag{1-3.3b}$$

The differences in the elapsed time for the motion of light through the ether in the three cases examined are in the second order (quadratic terms) of v/c. That is, these times differ in the difference between $(v/c)^2$ and 1. For the velocities with which the earth moves in its orbit, the quantity $(v/c)^2$ is about 10^{-8}. We must measure $\Delta t_{\parallel}$ and $\Delta t_{\perp}$ to a precision of at least one part in a hundred million if two separate measurements are to be made and compared.

However, a way around the difficulty was conceived by Albert A. Michelson (1852-1931), and in 1887 Michelson and Morley performed an experiment which should have been able to detect the motion of the earth through the ether, or put in another way, should have been able to test the applicability of the Galilean transformation to the motion of light. Michelson reasoned that a direct comparison of the parallel and perpendicular transit times might be made by using light waves as their own means of measuring time. Suppose we combine the parallel and perpendicular rods, as in Fig. 1-3.3. Then a beam of light from a source is split into two by a lightly silvered mirror, half the light moving

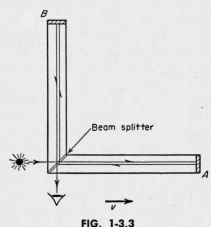

FIG. 1-3.3

down rod B and the other half down rod A. Upon reflection the light returns down the rods and can be inspected by an observer looking through the same mirror, but at $90°$ to the light source. Since the light is a wave motion, the two beams start out in phase, or in step. If the beams return in step, then the time required for the two trips is the same, but if they return out of step the time difference between the two trips is the time for half an oscillation. If the light combines in step, the observer notes that the view is bright, while if out of step the two waves cancel, and the view is dark.

It is easy to see that this apparatus might have the necessary precision. Yellow light, of wavelength 600 millimicrons (nanometers), has a period of 2×10^{-15} sec, so that the time for half an oscillation is about 10^{-15} sec. An interferometer in which the length of each section is about 15 m yields an elapsed time of 10^{-7} sec for the return trip. Thus a time measurement to half the period of oscillation of a light wave could measure the transit time to $10^{-15}/10^{-7}$, or to 1 part in 10^8, as required. In the actual experiment the path length employed was 11 m.

Since there was no independent way of determining that the length of the two paths was identical, the instrument was first adjusted to yield a bright view to the observer and then was rotated by $90°$. By this means any difference between the parallel and perpendicular transit times could be detected.

Although the design of the instrument showed that it was capable of detecting the time differences predicted by the Galilean transformation, no shift in the appearance of the field of view was detected which could be attributed to motion through the ether. The experiment was a failure, but this failure was one which in retrospect proved to be a great success.

The Michelson-Morley experiment was repeated many times, by different observers, using apparatus constructed of different materials, in different laboratories. Each time the experiment failed to detect the required difference in time for the light to traverse paths parallel and perpendicular to the earth's motion. Physicists, disturbed by these results, tried to grasp at straws.

It was supposed that the ether was dragged (convected) along the surface of the earth and for this reason no effect was found in the Michelson-Morley experiment. Other experiments were performed to detect the convected ether, without success.

An ingenious postulate proposed by H. A. Lorentz (1853-1928), and known as the *Lorentz contraction,* was that moving objects shrink in their direction of motion through the ether. If the amount of shrinkage was properly chosen, the times of flight in the two paths would be the same. Suppose that a rod at rest in the ether has a length L_0, and that a rod moving through the ether with its length aligned perpendicular to its direction of motion is unaltered, that is $L_\perp = L_0$. Then Eq. 1-3.1c gives the time $\Delta t_\perp$ correctly, provided that we replace L by $L_\perp$ or by L_0. If a rod moving through the ether and aligned parallel to its motion shrinks, with its new length given by

$$L_{||} = L_0(1 - v^2/c^2)^{1/2}, \qquad (1\text{-}3.4)$$

we would find that

$$\Delta t_{||} = \Delta t_\perp = \frac{2L_0}{c} \frac{1}{(1 - v^2/c^2)^{1/2}}. \qquad (1\text{-}3.5)$$

This result would account for the failure to detect a time difference in the two paths in the Michelson-Morley experiment.

These explanations had an unsatisfactory ring. Invented to explain away a negative experiment, they had no other detectable consequence than to explain the effect for which they were created.

But a train of thought was set into motion by the failure of the Michelson-Morley experiment to find an ether, culminating in the *Special Theory of Relativity* of Albert Einstein (1879-1956) in 1905, a theory that no physical experiment could detect the absolute motion of an inertial reference frame.

§1-4 The Special Theory of Relativity   In order to explain the results of the Michelson-Morley experiment, we might propose that nature behaves in a way we would not have anticipated, that the Galilean transformation is incorrect, and that velocities do not add vectorially (at high speeds). Following Einstein, we reason that there is no purpose in postulating the existence of an ether if there is no way to detect it; that is, if no physical experiment can detect the absolute motion of an inertial reference frame. Thus there is no purpose in speaking of a velocity of light except with respect to the observer who measures it. We reason further that no one observer has a special place, superior to all others. The speed of light should have the same numerical value for all observers, so long as they are all resident in inertial frames. We propose, as a fundamental postulate of the relativity theory, that *physical law must have the same meaning in all inertial frames.* This postulate is called the postulate of *covariance of physical law.*

As a first step in the application of the general principle, let us suppose that the constancy of the speed of light is a physical law; that is, the speed of light is the same in every inertial frame. Then the speed of light is the same in every direction and does not depend on the earth's speed through space or its speed with respect to an undetectable ether.

While the relativity principle quickly dispels the need for a convected ether and for the shrinkage of moving objects, it introduces other questions needing further exploration, for the principle seems to contradict ordinary experience. We will see that the relativity theory does not contradict ordinary experience. Rather it contradicts extrapolations from ordinary experience which are not ordinarily subjected to experimental test. While we know that the Galilean transformation is true in ordinary experience, we have no basis for assuming, without experimental test, that it is true at speeds comparable to the speed of light. We will require of statements of relativity that they agree with ordinary experience in the limit of low velocities. Whenever an experimental test has been made of deductions from the special theory of relativity, these deductions have been shown to be quantitatively correct. In consequence physicists have great confidence in relativity theory.

§1-5 The Rod Clock One consequence of the special theory of relativity that has aroused great popular interest lies in the measurement of time. Moving clocks do not run at the same rate as clocks fixed in the laboratory. We shall see that *moving clocks run slow*.

Let us design a clock, taking account of our new view of the speed of light. If the speed of light is constant, and has the same value for observers in any inertial frame, then in principle we have no need for independent measures of length and time. A clock may be made from a rod, as in Fig. 1-3.2: a rod of length L provided with a mirror at one end and provided at the other end with a pulsed light source and a detector with a fast trigger to the source. Such a system is an oscillator, or a *rod clock*. If the light source is initially flashed, the light will travel down the stick and back with speed c and be detected; the detector will then trigger the light source to flash again. The time interval between successive flashes is constant. In principle we may therefore define any two of the three quantities, the unit of length, the unit of time, or the speed of light, but not all three. At present it is simpler to define a fundamental unit of length and a fundamental unit of time, and to measure the speed of light, but there is no basic reason why this must always be so.

Consider a moving rod clock, as in Fig. 1-5.1, oriented trans-

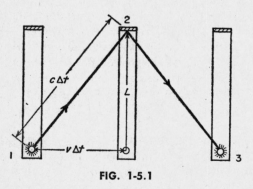

FIG. 1-5.1

verse to its direction of motion. Suppose that there is an observer in the coordinate frame in which the rod is at rest. We call this the *proper frame* of the rod. An observer in the proper frame of the rod will note that the light flashes in intervals of $2L/c$, assuming the detector to be infinitely fast. An observer in the laboratory notes that the path of the beam from the moving source to the moving mirror is not L long, but is from the source at position 1 to the mirror at position 2, and thence to the detector at position 3. For him Δt is the time from 1 to 2, so that the interval between flashes is $2\Delta t$, according to

$$c^2 \, \Delta t^2 = L^2 + v^2 \, \Delta t^2,$$

or

$$\Delta t = \frac{L}{c} \frac{1}{(1 - v^2/c^2)^{1/2}}.$$

Thus if $2\Delta t_0$ is the interval between flashes as determined by a proper observer (for whom the rod clock is at rest), we find that an observer in the laboratory frame, for whom the rod clock is moving with speed v transverse to the orientation of the rod, measures the time interval between flashes to be $2\Delta t$, and that these two are related by the equation

$$\Delta t = \Delta t_0 (1 - v^2/c^2)^{-1/2}. \tag{1-5.1}$$

In the literature of relativity it is customary to use the notation

$$v/c = \beta, \quad \text{and} \quad (1 - v^2/c^2)^{-1/2} = (1 - \beta^2)^{-1/2} = \gamma. \tag{1-5.2}$$

Note that the relations between β and γ resemble the relations between $\sin \theta$ and $\sec \theta$ in a right triangle whose hypotenuse is 1, and where the side opposite the angle θ is of length β. Then we have $\sin \theta = \beta$, $\sec \theta = \gamma$.

With the notation of Eq. 1-5.2, Eq. 1-5.1 becomes

$$\Delta t = \gamma \, \Delta t_0. \tag{1-5.3}$$

Now consider the meaning of the rod clock experiment. The laboratory observer and the moving observer both have rod clocks. Each observer knows his clock to keep correct time. Yet whichever is considered to be the observer at rest notes that the moving clock runs at an incorrect rate. Instead of measuring a time interval between flashes of $2\Delta t_0$ which the rest clock reads, the moving clock is observed by the rest observer to take a time $2\gamma\Delta t_0$ between flashes. The speed of a moving object is always less than c, so that γ is always greater than 1.

An observer in an inertial frame, comparing two clocks, one at rest with respect to his frame and the other moving with velocity v with respect to his frame, must conclude that the interval between flashes of the moving clock is longer than the corresponding interval of the rest clock. A clock consists of two parts, one which beats off time intervals, and the other which counts them. The counter in the laboratory which tallies the flashes of the moving clock will show fewer counts than the counter which tallies the flashes of the rest clock. The laboratory observer must conclude that moving clocks run slow.

While we have here discussed a rod clock, no restriction to this special model is implied. All clocks on a given inertial frame run at the same rate, if they are running correctly. All moving clocks run slow, whether these be rod clocks, or atomic clocks, or biological clocks, or any other kind.

1-5.1 Find γ for $\beta = $ 3/5, 4/5, 5/13, 12/13. Use the right triangle relationships. If $\sin \theta = \beta$, then $\sec \theta = \gamma$. [1.2, 1.67, 1.08, 2.6]

1-5.2 If $\beta = 1 - x$, then $\gamma^{-2} = 2x - x^2 \cong 2x$ for small x or for β close to 1. Prove that the error in γ in making the approximation that x^2 may be neglected in comparison to $2x$ is $-25x$ percent.

CHAPTER BIBLIOGRAPHY

P. Hume and D. Ivey, *Frames of Reference* (a film), Modern Learning Aids, New York.

Measurement of the Speed of Light (a film), McGraw-Hill Book Company, Inc., Text Film Department, New York.

R. S. Shankland, "Michelson Morley Experiment," Am. J. Phys. **32**, 16 (1964).

2   *The Lorentz Transformation*

§2-1   The Lorentz Transformation   We may consider a co-ordinate transformation between two inertial frames as a dictionary by whose means observers residing on the two frames can make their meaning clear to each other. In ordinary experience we need the assistance of the Galilean transformation to reconcile the determination of velocities on two inertial frames. An observer on the ground who measures the velocity of an airplane with respect to his frame will arrive at an entirely different result than the pilot reading his airspeed indicator and his compass heading. If these observers communicate by radio, their results are completely contradictory until the conflict is resolved through the Galilean transformation.

Consider the requirements upon a set of transformation equations which will fulfill our needs:

(1) The transformation must be linear; that is, a single event in one inertial frame must transform to a single event in another frame, with a single set of coordinates.

(2) The transformation must approach the Galilean transformation in the limit of low speeds. Here low speeds mean low compared to c, so that we wish to examine the transformation in the limit $\beta \rightarrow 0$.

(3) The speed of light must have the same value, c, in every inertial frame.

Just as the disturbance in a pond resulting from dropping a pebble into the water is a system of circular ripples, so a flash of light spreads out as a growing sphere. We may describe this sphere, whose radius grows at speed c, by the equation

$$x^2 + y^2 + z^2 = c^2 t^2. \qquad (2\text{-}1.1)$$

Just as the spreading light flash forms a spreading sphere in the unprimed frame, so it must also form a spreading sphere in the primed frame. Suppose the flash of light takes place at the instant when both t and t' are zero, and when the origins of the two frames coincide. Then the equation of the sphere of light in the primed frame must be

$$x'^2 + y'^2 + z'^2 = c^2 t'^2. \qquad (2\text{-}1.2)$$

The coordinate transformation that satisfies these requirements is called the Lorentz transformation, after its discoverer, and forms the mathematical beginning of the special theory of relativity. The space and time coordinates of an event recorded in two inertial frames whose axes are parallel, and whose origins coincide at time zero (in both frames), are related by the equations

$$x' = \gamma(x - Vt), \qquad \text{and conversely} \quad x = \gamma(x' + Vt'); \qquad (2\text{-}1.3)$$
$$y' = y, \qquad\qquad\qquad\qquad\qquad y = y';$$
$$z' = z, \qquad\qquad\qquad\qquad\qquad z = z';$$
$$t' = \gamma(t - Vx/c^2), \qquad\qquad\quad t = \gamma(t' + Vx'/c^2).$$

In these equations the primed frame is taken to be moving with speed V in the $+x$ direction with respect to the unprimed frame. Conversely the unprimed frame may be taken to be moving with speed V in the $-x'$ direction with respect to the primed frame. As indicated in Eqs. 1-5.2, we use the symbol $\gamma = (1 - V^2/c^2)^{-1/2}$.

The Lorentz transformation fulfills the first two requirements we have stated. It is linear, and in the limit $V \to 0$, $\gamma \to 1$, the Eqs. 2-1.3 become the Galilean transformation, Eqs. 1-2.1; the Lorentz transformation yields the results of ordinary experience in the limit of low velocities.

By direct substitution of Eqs. 2-1.3 into the equation of the light sphere in the unprimed frame, Eq. 2-1.1, we find the equation of the light sphere in the primed frame.

Thus the Lorentz transformation fulfills requirement (3) above. A pulse of light emitted at the coincident origin of the two frames spreads out as a sphere in both frames. When observers in the unprimed frame translate their observations to the language of the primed frame, the translated observation is in agreement with observations of the primed observers, that a light sphere spreads out from the origin of the primed coordinates with speed c.

2-1.1 By direct application of the Lorentz transformation equations, show that Eq. 2-1.1 is transformed into Eq. 2-1.2.

2-1.2 By taking differentials of the Lorentz transformation equations, show that the quantity ds transforms to ds', where $ds^2 = dx^2 + dy^2 + dz^2 - c^2dt^2$, and $ds'^2 = dx'^2 + dy'^2 + dz'^2 - c^2dt'^2$.

§2-2 Simultaneity and Time Sequence Suppose we now examine some implications of the Lorentz transformations. Let there be as many observers in each inertial frame as are required. Observers in each frame have access to identical meter sticks, and to identical clocks. They use identical procedures in their measurements. Each measured event is described at least by a set of four coordinates, giving the position and time at which the event took place.

In any inertial frame the clocks of all observers are synchronized. They have been checked by stationing a third observer midway between any two. He notes that the pair of clocks reads the same. This procedure takes account of the finite speed of light, and insures that there are no alterations in the clock's behavior, as there might be if they were carried to a central timing station.

In any one frame there is no doubt as to when two events are simultaneous, wherever they occur. If two events occur at the same time, the same reading of the clocks located at the places where the events occurred assures us that the events were simultaneous.

Let us consider two events, 1 and 2, which are simultaneous in the unprimed frame. Then $t_1 = t_2$, wherever the events took place. But whether they are noted as simultaneous in the primed frame depends on where the events took place. From the Lorentz transformation, Eqs. 3-1.3, we note that

$$t'_1 = \gamma(t_1 - Vx_1/c^2) \quad \text{and} \quad t'_2 = \gamma(t_2 - Vx_2/c^2).$$

The difference between the time of the two events in the primed frame is

$$t'_2 - t'_1 = \frac{\gamma V}{c^2}(x_1 - x_2). \tag{2-2.1}$$

Two events simultaneous in the unprimed frame are observed to be simultaneous in the primed frame only if they occur at the same point, $x_1 = x_2$. The second event might appear earlier, or later than the first, depending on the value of their x coordinates.

Suppose now that the event t_1 was first, and t_2 was second, in the unprimed frame. The time difference between them may be obtained from the above equations as

$$t'_2 - t'_1 = \gamma \left[(t_2 - t_1) - \frac{V}{c^2}(x_2 - x_1) \right]. \tag{2-2.2}$$

If the quantity in brackets is equal to zero, then the two events are simultaneous in the primed frame. If greater than zero, then the events are observed in the primed frame in the same order as in the unprimed frame. If less than zero, then the events are observed in reverse order. The last case can arise only if

$$x_2 - x_1 > c(t_2 - t_1),$$

that is, if the two events happen at such remote places that a ray of light leaving event 1 could not have reached point 2 in time to cause event 2. We say that the time sequence of two events can only be inverted if they could not have been "causally connected"; that is, if event 1 could conceivably have caused event 2 (by sending a radio signal, or by tripping a switch), then the order of the events cannot be inverted. No signal can travel faster than the speed of light, so that if a light beam could not bridge the interval between the two events the second event could not have had knowledge of the prior occurrence of the first.

2-2.1 Two light bulbs in the laboratory, one at $x = 0$ and the other at $x = 10$ km, are set to flash simultaneously at $t = 0$. Observers on a magic carpet moving in the $+x$ direction with speed 3×10^7 m/sec observe the flashes. (a) What time interval do they note between flashes?

(b) Which bulb do they say goes off first? [(a) 3.34×10^{-9} sec (b) the bulb at 10 km]

2-2.2 A long straight rod is inclined at angle θ to the x axis. The rod moves in the y direction with velocity V. (a) Find the velocity v with which the point of intersection of the rod and the x-axis moves along the x axis. (b) If $V = 10^{10}$ cm/sec, and $\theta = 0.10$ rad, what is the numerical value of v? (c) Does your result contradict the relativistic demand that c is a limiting speed for all material particles? [(a) $v = V \cot \theta$ (b) 10^{11} cm/sec (c) no, for the point of intersection of the ruler with the x axis is a mathematical point rather than a material particle.]

§2-3 Time Dilation Suppose we examine, from the vantage point of the laboratory (the unprimed frame), a clock which is stationary in the primed frame. The primed frame is the proper frame of the clock, for this is the frame in which the clock is at rest. The clock then is moving with speed V in the $+x$ direction with respect to the laboratory.

Since the clock is in fixed x' position, the time interval between two beats of the clock at t'_1 and t'_2 will appear in the laboratory frame to be

$$t_2 - t_1 = \gamma(t'_2 - t'_1), \qquad (2\text{-}3.1)$$

by application of the Lorentz transformation, Eqs. 2-1.3, for $x'_2 = x'_1$. We may therefore set $x'_2 = x'_1 = 0$ if we wish, for nothing is changed if the clock is at the origin of the primed coordinates.

This is the same result that we have obtained earlier for the rod clock, §1-5, in a slightly different notation. But here the result does not depend on the detailed design of the clock.

One variety of subatomic particles, called mesons, decays at an exponential rate such that $1/e$ of the original number remains after 2.6×10^{-8} sec, in a coordinate frame in which the mesons are at rest. Beams of π mesons may be produced by bombarding the target of an accelerator with high energy protons; the resulting mesons move out of the target at a speed which can be $0.99c$. In their proper frame π mesons decay at their proper rate, but laboratory observers measuring the decay rate of the moving mesons must find that the meson clocks run slow. From Eq. 2-3.1

the decay time will be measured in the laboratory to be $2.6 \times 10^{-8} \times (1 - 0.99^2)^{-1/2}$ sec, or 1.87×10^{-7} sec. In that time a meson beam moving with a speed of nearly 3×10^8 m/sec will move a distance of 56 m. Thus in 56 m the meson beam will drop to $1/e$ of its initial intensity. If this relativistic effect did not exist, we would expect the intensity of the beam to drop by $1/e$ each 2.6×10^{-8} sec in the laboratory, regardless of the motion. Since in this case $\gamma = 7.18$, we would here have expected the beam to drop by $e^{-7.18}$, or to drop to $1/1300$ of its initial intensity in 56 m. The difference between $1/1300$ and $1/e = 1/2.78$ is readily detected. Time dilation is thus confirmed in the laboratory, and is today routinely taken for granted in the design of experiments which must be performed with particle beams in high-energy accelerators.

Let us repeat once again what we mean by time dilation. We mean that a proper time interval is dilated or expanded when measured from some inertial frame other than the proper frame. The proper frame is the frame in which the events took place at a single point. There is no change in any proper frame by virtue of its motion with respect to another frame. In fact it is one of the basic principles of the special theory of relativity that there is no physical effect which can be associated with the motion of an inertial frame. Such a motion cannot be detected by measurements wholly within that frame. It is impossible to build a completely self-contained speedometer which measures the motion of an inertial frame, except by reference to a second frame.

2-3.1 A particle with a mean proper lifetime of 1 μsec moves through the laboratory at 2.7×10^{10} cm/sec. (a) What is its lifetime, as measured by observers in the laboratory? (b) If it was manufactured in the target of an accelerator, how far does it go, on the average, in the laboratory before disintegrating? (c) Repeat the calculation of the preceding part without taking relativity into account. [(a) 2.3 μsec (b) 6.2×10^4 cm (c) 2.7×10^4 cm]

§2-4 Lorentz Contraction Let us set up an imaginary experiment to measure the length of a fixed rod and the length of a moving rod. There is no problem in measuring the length of a rod which is at rest in a coordinate frame. Observers in the frame simply note the coordinates of the ends of the rod, at their convenience, and apply the Pythagorean theorem to determine the length. Or, more simply, they might line up the rod with the x axis, and take the difference in the x coordinates of the ends of the rod as the length. But how do we measure the length of a moving rod?

Suppose we put observers everywhere along the x axis in the laboratory frame when the rod is moving in the $+x$ direction with speed V and is aligned parallel to the x axis. We ask the observers to synchronize their watches, and then to give some signal if the end of the rod is at their coordinate position at a predetermined time. The difference in the coordinates of the two observers in the laboratory frame who signal that they see opposite ends of the rod at the appointed time is to be taken as the length of the rod.

The results of the length measurement clearly depend on the meaning of simultaneity. Depending on the choice of the recipe for synchronizing watches, the rod could turn out to have any length at all. The relativistic recipe has already been chosen, and has been incorporated into the Lorentz transformation. We compare the coordinates of the ends of the rod in the primed and unprimed frames at the same laboratory (unprimed) time. From Eqs. 2-1.3 we find

$$x'_2 = \gamma(x_2 - Vt) \quad \text{and} \quad x'_1 = \gamma(x_1 - Vt),$$

which we subtract:

$$x'_2 - x'_1 = \gamma(x_2 - x_1). \tag{2-4.1}$$

On the left of Eq. 2-4.1 we have the difference in the coordinates of the ends of the rod as determined in the primed frame, the proper frame of the rod. On the right the difference in the coordinates of the ends of the rod as determined in the laboratory frame appear. Let us make the identifications

$$x'_2 - x'_1 = L' \quad \text{and} \quad x_2 - x_1 = L,$$

so that we have

$$L' = \gamma L. \qquad (2\text{-}4.2)$$

Remembering that γ is at least 1, we find that the measured length of the rod in the laboratory frame, L, is less than its proper length L' by the factor γ. This effect is today called the *Lorentz contraction*, for the formula with which Lorentz attempted to explain the negative result of the Michelson-Morley experiment is precisely the same as we have found here, though the interpretation of the formula is now different from his.

Notice that we do not require that rods shrink in their direction of motion for a proper observer, for whom the rod is at rest, as Lorentz proposed. Relativity requires that the contraction is related to the act of measurement. The way in which we set up to measure the length of a moving rod determines that we will measure a shorter length than the rod length. We would not have come to such a conclusion if the speed of light were infinite, for then β would be zero and the Lorentz transformation would be identical to the Galilean transformation. It is the finite speed of light which gives rise to these results.

Is the moving rod *really* contracted in its direction of motion? Is time *really* dilated? These questions depend on what is meant by *really*. In physics what is real is identical with what is measured. There is no way to assign properties to a rod or to a clock or to an electron except through measurement. In this sense the phenomena we have discussed as time dilation and the Lorentz contraction are real. But a physicist tries to unite his observations into a concise set of ideas. He measures the lifetime of π mesons at rest and in motion and finds it appropriate to combine these measurements into a *proper lifetime*, for all other lifetimes are easily calculable from this one. In general it is the proper length or the proper lifetime which one assigns to the meson or the rod. But in the laboratory moving mesons are *really* alive long after their twins, born at the same time, and at rest, are *really* dead.

2-4.1   A rod has a length of 1 m. When the rod is in a satellite moving with respect to the earth at $0.99c$, what is the length of the rod as determined by an observer in the satellite? [1 m]

2-4.2 A vector represented in coordinate form in the primed frame is given as $8\ \mathbf{1}_{x'} + 6\ \mathbf{1}_{y'}$. Find its representation in the unprimed frame, if the primed frame moves at $\mathbf{V} = 0.75c\ \mathbf{1}_x$ with respect to the unprimed frame. [$5.3\ \mathbf{1}_x + 6\ \mathbf{1}_y$]

2-4.3 A thin rod of length L_0 when measured by a proper observer is moving at $0.75c$ with respect to a second observer in a direction at $37°$ to its own length. What is the length L of the rod as measured by the second observer and his assistants? [$0.8\ L_0$]

§2-5 Velocity Transformations To find the Lorentz transformations of the velocities we employ the same technique we have used before, in the case of the Galilean transformation, §1-2. By taking differentials of Eqs. 2-1.3 we find

$$dx' = \gamma(dx - V\,dt), \qquad \text{and} \qquad dx = \gamma(dx' + V\,dt'); \qquad (2\text{-}5.1a)$$

$$dy' = dy, \qquad\qquad dy = dy'; \qquad (2\text{-}5.1b)$$

$$dz' = dz, \qquad\qquad dz = dz'; \qquad (2\text{-}5.1c)$$

$$dt' = \gamma(dt - V\,dx/c^2), \qquad dt' = \gamma(dt' + V\,dx'/c^2). \qquad (2\text{-}5.1d)$$

When we divide each of the first three equations in each column by the fourth equation of that column, we find

$$U'_x = \frac{U_x - V}{1 - \dfrac{U_x V}{c^2}}, \qquad \text{and} \qquad U_x = \frac{U'_x + V}{1 + \dfrac{U'_x V}{c^2}}; \qquad (2\text{-}5.2a)$$

$$U'_{y,z} = \frac{U_{y,z}}{\gamma\left(1 - \dfrac{U_x V}{c^2}\right)}, \qquad U_{y,z} = \frac{U'_{y,z}}{\gamma\left(1 + \dfrac{U'_x V}{c^2}\right)}. \qquad (2\text{-}5.2b)$$

In these equations we have written $U_x = \dfrac{dx}{dt}$, $U'_x = \dfrac{dx'}{dt'}$, and so on. U_x is the x component of the velocity of the particle as measured in the unprimed frame. U'_x is the x' component of the velocity of the particle as measured in the primed frame. The subscript y,z refers to either the y or the z component. In Eqs. 2-5.2 the primed frame is moving in the $+x$ direction with respect to the unprimed frame with speed V.

Note that Eqs. 2-5.2 reduce to the Galilean velocity transformations of Eqs. 1-2.3 in the nonrelativistic limit $\beta \to 0$. But there is a significant difference at large velocities. If the moving object is a photon moving in the primed frame with speed c in the $+x$ direction, and if the primed frame moves with speed c with respect to the unprimed frame, then

$$U_x = \frac{c + c}{1 + \dfrac{c^2}{c^2}} = c.$$

The speed of light is c in all inertial frames, whatever their relative speed. By the Galilean transformation we would have expected $U_x = 2c$, but we know that this is not applicable. Regardless of the value of V, if $U'_x = c$, then $U_x = c$. Of course this is how it must be, for the condition that the speed of light is c in all inertial frames is built into the Lorentz transformation.

2-5.1 (a) Two particles come toward each other, each with speed $0.9c$ with respect to the laboratory. What is their relative speed? (b) Two particles are emitted from a disintegrating source, each moving with speed $0.9c$ with respect to the source. What is their speed relative to each other? [(a) and (b) $0.995c$]

2-5.2 A particle has velocity $\mathbf{U}' = 3\ \mathbf{1}_{x'} + 4\ \mathbf{1}_{y'} + 12\ \mathbf{1}_{z'}$ m/sec in a coordinate frame which itself moves in the $+x$ direction with respect to the laboratory at $V = 0.8c$. Find $\mathbf{U}$ in the laboratory frame. [$\mathbf{U} = 2.4 \times 10^8\mathbf{1}_x + 2.4\ \mathbf{1}_y + 7.2\ \mathbf{1}_z$) m/sec]

§2-6 The Fizeau Experiment How can we detect evidence of the velocity transformation formulas in the laboratory? We have already seen that the speed of light in vacuum is c in every inertial frame, but what about its speed in a medium, such as water? The speed of light in a medium must clearly be with respect to a coordinate frame fixed in the medium, for the very structure of the medium, the position of its atoms and molecules, provides a preferred reference frame. The speed of light in a medium is less than c, and the index of refraction for a particular wavelength is $n = c/v$, a number generally greater than one.

If the medium is in motion with respect to the laboratory, at speed V, then the speed of light with respect to the laboratory U

will be different from its speed with respect to the medium U', according to Eqs. 2-5.2. If the light moves *parallel* to the motion of the medium and in the same direction, then its speed with respect to the laboratory is increased to U_p, while if the light moves *antiparallel* to the motion of the medium its speed with respect to the laboratory is reduced to U_a, both given from Eqs. 2-5.2 as

$$U_p = \frac{U' + V}{1 + \dfrac{U'V}{c^2}} \quad \text{and} \quad U_a = \frac{U' - V}{1 - \dfrac{U'V}{c^2}}. \qquad (2\text{-}6.1)$$

Consider the time difference between the transit times of two beams moving in opposite directions through a moving medium for a distance L as measured in the laboratory. The beams will take times whose difference Δt is given by

$$\Delta t = \frac{L}{U_p} - \frac{L}{U_a} = L \left(\frac{1 + U'V/c^2}{U' + V} - \frac{1 - U'V/c^2}{U' - V} \right). \qquad (2\text{-}6.2)$$

Suppose we have beams of yellow light moving in opposite directions through flowing water. As a practical case let us take the path to be $L = 15$ m, $U' = 0.7c$ (for the refractive index of water is about 1.5), and $V = 3$ m/sec $= 10^{-8}c$, for the steady flow of water in a tube. We find

$$\Delta t = 15m \left(\frac{1 + 0.7 \times 10^{-8}}{0.7c + 10^{-8}c} - \frac{1 - 0.7 \times 10^{-8}}{0.7c - 10^{-8}c} \right)$$

$$= \frac{15m}{2.1 \times 10^8 \text{ m/sec}} (2 \times 0.7 \times 10^{-8})$$

$$= 10^{-15} \text{ sec.}$$

This time is about the time for half an oscillation of yellow light, as we saw in §1-3 in our discussion of the Michelson-Morley experiment. In an analogous way a beam of light can be split and the separate parts sent two ways around a tube of flowing water, as in Fig. 2-6.1. If the system is inspected when the water is at rest, then a readily detectable difference in the appearance of the image may be observed when the flow is turned on, in quantita-

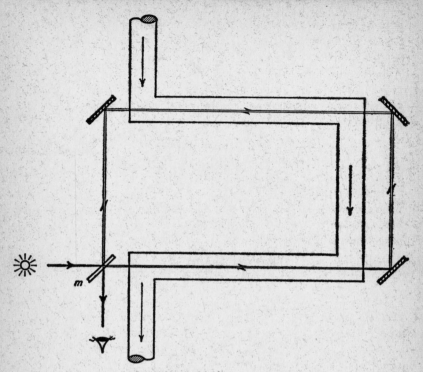

FIG. 2-6.1   Fizeau experiment. Light from a source is split by a lightly silvered mirror at *m*. One beam passes through the flowing fluid in a direction parallel to the flow, and the other in a direction antiparallel to the flow.

tive agreement with our calculations. This experiment was first performed by Fizeau (1819-1896) in 1851.

§2-7 Aberration   In 1726 Bradley first observed that distant stars lying perpendicular to the plane of the earth's orbit describe a small, nearly circular, annual orbit, 41″ in angular diameter. As shown in Fig. 2-7.1, the telescope must be pointed away from the normal to the orbit, into the direction of the earth's motion, as though to let the light fall through. This phenomenon is

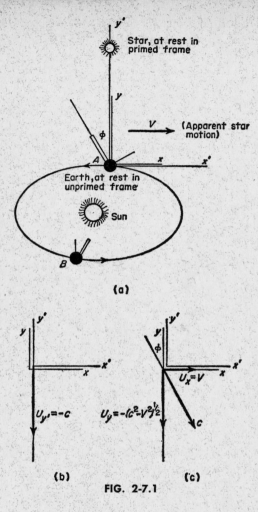

FIG. 2-7.1

wholly understandable in terms of the velocity transformation equations.

If the proper frame of the star is the primed frame, the components of the velocity of the starlight reaching the earth in this frame are $U'_y = c$, $U'_x = 0$, $U'_z = 0$, to a sufficient approximation. When the earth is at position A, Fig. 2-7.1a, and moving with speed V with respect to the sun, then according to our notation we think of the primed frame as moving in the $+x$ direction with speed V with respect to the unprimed frame. From Eqs. 2-5.2 we find the components of the speed of light in the unprimed (earth's) frame as

$$U_x = V, \quad U_y = -c\gamma^{-1} = -(c^2 - v^2)^{1/2}, \quad U_z = 0. \quad (2\text{-}7.1)$$

The resultant of these components is c, Fig. 2-7.1c. The direction of the resultant is the direction in which the light will be seen to come when the earth is at A. At B the tilt of the telescope must be as indicated, differently from its orientation at A, and again so as to "catch the light."

From Fig. 2-7.1c we have

$$\sin \phi = v/c. \quad (2\text{-}7.2)$$

Thus the earth's speed can be measured through the stellar aberration provided that we know the speed of light. Taking $c = 3 \times 10^8$ m/sec and $\phi = 20.5''$, we find $V = 30$ km/sec. Aberration furnishes independent proof that the earth revolves about the sun, and not the sun around the earth. Knowing the earth's speed and the length of the year, we can find the circumference of the earth's orbit, and thus the distance from the earth to the sun.

Aberration is also of importance in high-energy physics. Rapidly moving protons in the cosmic rays enter the earth's atmosphere and are decelerated, radiating light. Particles accelerated in high-energy accelerators move in curved paths, being centripetally accelerated in this deflection; they thereby radiate electromagnetic energy. In both cases this radiation is predominantly in the forward direction of the motion, as seen in the laboratory. This bunching of the radiant energy in the forward direction results from aberration, and is known as the *headlight effect*.

Suppose a source of radiation radiates energy uniformly in all directions in its proper frame (the primed frame), as shown in Fig. 2-7.2. The source moves in the $+x$ direction with respect to

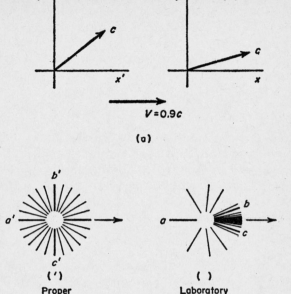

FIG. 2-7.2 Headlight effect [After V. F. Weisskopf, Physics Today 13, 24 (1960)].

the laboratory frame (the unprimed frame) with speed V. Radiation emitted at an angle θ' with respect to the x' axis will be observed to make an angle θ with respect to the x axis. We find this angle by noting that $U'_x = c \cos \theta'$ and $U_x = c \cos \theta$, and substituting these values into Eq. 2-5.2a for the transformation of the x component of the velocity, which gives

$$\cos \theta = \frac{\cos \theta' + \beta}{1 + \beta \cos \theta'}. \qquad (2\text{-}7.3)$$

On Fig. 2-7.2b we have mapped corresponding rays in the primed and unprimed frames, when $\beta = 0.9$, using Eq. 2-7.3.

When θ' is 0 or π, then θ has the same values, but when $\theta' = \pm \pi/2$ we find cos $\theta' = 0$ so that cos $\theta = 0.9$ and $\theta = \pm 25°$, and so on. The rays are strongly concentrated in the forward direction with very little radiation coming off in the backward direction, as seen in the laboratory. It is this effect that we have called the headlight effect. The bunching of radiation in the direction of motion may be observed in the radiation from accelerated charged particles in the machines of high energy physics, where it is called *synchrotron radiation*. The radiation may be observed as visible light by looking into the direction of motion of the beam.

2-7.1   At what speed does an observer have to move toward a star in order that half the radiation emitted by the star is concentrated within a cone subtending an angle of 0.01 radian. Approximate cos θ as $1 - \theta^2/2 + \cdots$. [$0.9995c$]

2-7.2   Prove that the aberration angle in Fig. 2-7.1 would be given by tan $\theta = v/c$ if the Galilean transformation were correct.

§2-8 Visual Appearance of Rapidly Moving Objects   When we discuss the effect of the Lorentz transformation we must be clear about the meaning of "observing" and "seeing." Up to this point we have been careful to use the word observe, as in connection with the Lorentz contraction, instead of the word see.

Let us consider in detail the manner in which laboratory observers determine the length of a moving rod, or the time interval between flashes of a moving clock. First we must station a set of observers everywhere in the laboratory frame. Of course, if the motion is along the x axis, we only need observers along the x axis. Then we instruct these observers to note their coordinates and synchronize their clocks. If we wish to measure the length of a moving rod, we instruct the observers to note whether or not an end of the rod was at their coordinate position at a predetermined time. The difference in the coordinates of the two observers who are coincident with an end of the rod is defined as the length of the moving rod. If we wish to measure the interval between flashes of a moving clock, as the rod clock, we ask laboratory observers to note whether they were coincident with the moving clock at the time it flashed, and if so what was the reading on their own clock at the time the moving clock flashed. The difference between the times read by two laboratory observers is the laboratory time interval which corresponds to the time interval on the moving clock. This is the meaning of the operations in the experimental determination of the Lorentz contraction and of the time-dilation phenomena. This is the meaning of the word observe.

By seeing, or by photographing, we mean something else. The difference is most clear in connection with photography. When we take a photograph, there is only one lens. When we see, there is only one observer. The difference between observing and seeing is the difference between an infinity of observers and one observer.

In the operations we call observing we have taken care that there is no time required for the passage of a light signal from the event to the laboratory observer who detects it. The operation of seeing is quite different. The observer is at one location in the laboratory frame, and the events he notes may have taken ages to reach him. A telescope camera photographing distant stars during a solar eclipse may have its shutter open a very short time. The light which enters the shutter may come from distant stars, having been emitted millions of years ago, and during the same exposure the shutter may admit light from the solar corona emitted 500 sec ago, and even light from an adjacent clock emitted nanoseconds ago. We may imagine the camera lens or the eye to be at the center of a collapsing spherical shell, which collapses at the speed of light and collects events as it goes. If an event takes place in the time interval during which the shell passes, information about the event is swept along by the shell and will be recorded by the camera.

In spite of inferences that might be drawn incorrectly from a casual inspection of the Lorentz contraction, a careful consideration of the picture-taking process leads to the conclusion that pictures of rapidly moving distant objects are undistorted in shape. But the picture taken in the laboratory from one direction will be the same as obtained in the proper frame, but from a different vantage point, as we might expect from our discussion of aberration in §2-7.

Suppose a cube of edge l is moving with speed V in the $+x$

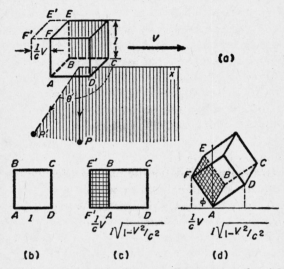

FIG. 2-8.1 Visual appearance of a rapidly moving cube: (a) the moving cube; (b) a proper photograph from point P; (c) the laboratory photographer's picture from P; (d) the laboratory photographer's interpretation of his picture. In (a) the point P' is the point from which the proper photographer would obtain the same picture as (c), which the laboratory photographer took from P [After V. F. Weisskopf, Physics Today 13, 24 (1960)].

direction, and that it is photographed from a distant point P (see Fig. 2-8.1a). A camera in the laboratory frame and one in the proper frame will take different pictures, even when both pictures are taken from the same point. The two pictures are shown in Fig. 2-8.1b and c. In the laboratory frame the camera collects light from the back edge EF as well as from the front face $ABCD$, for light emitted from the back edge at a time l/c before light from the front face was emitted will arrive at the camera at the same time as light from the front face, for all this light will be swept up in the same collapsing light shell. At that earlier time the rear edge was at $E'F'$, displaced from the present position EF by Vl/c. By the Lorentz contraction the front face will be contracted so that the edge AB will be measured to be of length l $(1 - V^2/c^2)^{1/2}$. The laboratory photographer's picture will be as in Fig. 2-8.1c instead of Fig. 2-8.1b, which is the picture taken by a proper photographer from point P. But the laboratory photographer will infer that the cube has rotated through an angle $\phi = \cos^{-1} \beta$, as shown in Fig. 2-8.1d. Note that this is the same picture that a proper photographer would have taken from a different orientation, as at P' in Fig. 2-8.1a.

Although the discussion above was based on a cube, it is clear that the apparent rotation must be the same for all rapidly moving distant objects. Photographs of rapidly moving distant objects will not show the Lorentz contraction. A spherical rocket ship will look spherical, as if it were photographed from the side in the proper frame. The picture that one would obtain in the proper frame at an angle θ' with **V** is the same picture which would be taken in the laboratory at an angle θ with **V**, as in Eq. 2-7.3 for the aberration of light. In the figure we have taken $\theta = \pi/2$, so that from Eq. 2-7.3 $\cos \theta' = -\beta$ and θ' is greater than $\pi/2$, as shown.

2-8.1 A small object is in the form of a sphere of radius R in its proper frame. Determine the shape of the particle (a) as measured (observed) by a set of observers in the laboratory frame, and (b) as photographed by a photographer in the laboratory frame when the particle moves at $V = 0.5c$ in the $+x$ direction with respect to the laboratory. [(a) ellipsoidal: $4x^2/3 + y^2 + z^2 = R^2$ (b) spherical]

2-8.2 A cube oriented with its edges parallel to the coordinate axes moves in the $+x$ direction at $V = 0.6c$, and a picture is taken when the cube passes the origin by a distant observer located along the $-y$ axis. At what angle with respect to **V** would a photographer in the proper frame have to be located to take the same picture? [127°]

§2-9 **Transformation of Acceleration**   If we take differentials of the velocity transformation equations (2-5.2), we find that

$$dU_x = \frac{dU'_x}{1 + VU'_x/c^2} - \frac{V + U'_x}{(1 + VU'_x/c^2)^2} \frac{V}{c^2} dU'_x, \qquad (2\text{-}9.1a)$$

$$dU_{y,z} = \frac{dU'_{y,z}}{\gamma(1 + VU'_x/c^2)} - \frac{U'_{y,z}}{\gamma(1 + VU'_x/c^2)^2} \frac{V}{c^2} dU'_{y,z}. \qquad (2\text{-}9.1b)$$

We will restrict ourselves to the case where the particle is instantaneously at rest in the proper frame; that is,

$$U'_x = U'_y = U'_z = 0,$$

but the instantaneous acceleration is not necessarily zero in the proper frame. In this case Eqs. 2-9.1 become

$$dU_x = dU'_x(1 - V^2/c^2) = dU'_x\gamma^{-2}, \qquad (2\text{-}9.2a)$$

and $$dU_{y,z} = dU'_{y,z}\gamma^{-1}. \qquad (2\text{-}9.2b)$$

To find the transformation equations for the acceleration we must divide Eqs. 2-9.2 by an appropriate equation relating time differentials in the two systems. From the Lorentz transformation equations (2-1.3) we have

$$t = \gamma(t' - Vx'/c^2),$$

and, taking differentials,

$$dt = \gamma(dt' - V\,dx'/c^2),$$

or $$dt = \gamma\,dt'\left(1 - \frac{V}{c^2}\frac{dx'}{dt'}\right).$$

Since we have set ourselves the limitation that $U'_x = \dfrac{dx'}{dt'} = 0$, the preceding equation becomes

$$dt = \gamma\,dt'. \qquad (2\text{-}9.3)$$

Dividing each of Eqs. 2-9.2 by 2-9.3, we obtain the transformation equations for the acceleration as

$$a_x = \frac{dU_x}{dt} = \frac{1}{\gamma^3}\frac{dU'_x}{dt'} = \gamma^{-3}a'_x, \qquad (2\text{-}9.4a)$$

$$a_{y,z} = \frac{dU_{y,z}}{dt} = \frac{1}{\gamma^2}\frac{dU'_{y,z}}{dt'} = \gamma^{-2}a'_{y,z}. \qquad (2\text{-}9.4b)$$

Equations 2-9.4 are transformation equations for the acceleration in the special case that the particle is instantaneously at rest (but may be accelerating) in the primed frame. We will have no need in this book for the more general equations of transformation which could be derived from Eqs. 2-9.1.

In the Galilean transformation the acceleration of a particle is the same in all inertial frames. This is not true at high velocities where the Lorentz transformation applies. Accelerations in one frame differ in magnitude and direction from the accelerations measured in another inertial frame. This is due to the Lorentz contraction and to time dilation.

If we make use of the binomial expansion of $(1 + x)^m$, as in Eq. 1-3.2, we find that

$$\gamma^{-2} = (1 - V^2/c^2),$$

and $\qquad \gamma^{-3} = (1 - V^2/c^2)^{3/2} = 1 - \frac{3}{2}\frac{V^2}{c^2} + \cdots .$

Thus to terms of the second order in V/c the Galilean transformation is correct. So long as we can neglect V^2/c^2 compared to 1 we need not concern ourselves with differences in the acceleration as measured on different inertial frames. These terms do become important in our analysis of the behavior of electrons and protons in electric and magnetic fields.

It is sometimes convenient to rewrite Eqs. 2-9.4 so as not to make specific reference to an axis system. We replace the subscript x by one which indicates that we are considering a component parallel to the motion of the particle as observed from the laboratory frame. We replace the subscripts y,z by one which indicates that the component is perpendicular to the motion. Thus we may write

$$a_{\|} = a'_{\|}\gamma^{-3}, \qquad (2\text{-}9.5a)$$

and $\qquad a_{\perp} = a'_{\perp}\gamma^{-2}. \qquad (2\text{-}9.5b)$

2-9.1 A particle experiences an acceleration of $\mathbf{a}' = (3\,\mathbf{1}_{x'} + 4\,\mathbf{1}_{y'} + 12$

$1_{z'}$) cm/sec^2 in a coordinate frame in which it is instantaneously at rest. What is its acceleration as measured in the laboratory, if the instantaneous proper frame of the particle is moving at $V = 0.98c$ 1_x with respect to the laboratory? [$a = (0.024$ $1_x + 0.16$ $1_y + 0.48$ $1_z)$ cm/sec^2, $a = 0.51$ cm/sec^2]

2-9.2 A particle experiences an acceleration of $a' = (3$ $1_{x'} + 4$ $1_{y'})$ cm/sec^2 in a coordinate frame in which it is instantaneously at rest. Find (a) the magnitude of the acceleration, and (b) the direction it makes with the x' axis. The particle is observed to move in the $+x$ direction at $0.98c$ in the laboratory frame. Find (c) the acceleration as measured in the laboratory, and (d) the angle the acceleration makes with the x axis in the laboratory frame. [(a) 5 cm/sec^2 (b) 37° (c) 0.038 cm/sec^2 (d) 81.4°]

CHAPTER BIBLIOGRAPHY

R. P. Durbin, H. H. Loar, and W. W. Havens, "The Lifetimes of π^+ and π^- Mesons," Phys. Rev. **88**, 179 (1952).

D. H. Frisch and J. H. Smith, "Measurement of Relativistic Time Dilation Using μ Mesons," Am. J. Phys. **31**, 342 (1963).

D. H. Frisch, J. H. Smith, and F. L. Friedman, *Time Dilation* (a film), Educational Services Inc., Watertown, Mass.

J. Terrell, "Invisibility of Lorentz Contraction," Phys. Rev. **116**, 1041 (1959).

V. F. Weisskopf, "The Visual Appearance of Rapidly Moving Objects," Physics Today **13**, 24 (1960).

3 Force and Motion

§3-1 Introduction For many centuries motions have been analyzed in terms of forces. Long before Galileo and Newton, motions were classified as natural or violent. It was thought that natural motions took place without the application of an outside force, while violent motions required the application of a force. Different conditions seemed to prevail on earth and in heaven. For heavenly bodies the natural state seemed to be circular motion, for wherever one looked there were circles: the sun was circular, the moon was bounded by circles, the planets were circular, and the stars seemed to describe circular paths. On the surface of the earth, and for horizontal motions, a state of rest seemed the natural state, for objects came to rest when left by themselves, while vertical motions like those of falling bodies seemed natural ones.

The analysis we call *Newtonian mechanics* is based on a similar conceptual structure. Motions are analyzed in terms of forces. But the concept of a natural motion is somewhat more abstract. Newton's first law expresses the motion a body will describe if left alone, the natural motion, as one either of rest or of uniform motion in a straight line. According to Newton there is one universal natural state, equally valid on earth and in heaven, equally valid for vertical and for horizontal motions. In Newtonian mechanics no force is required to maintain an object in uniform motion in a straight line. It is the departure from uniform motion in a straight line that requires a force. Recall that for earlier formulations a force was required for departure from a state of rest.

Developments in physics in the past 50 or 75 years have limited the realm of validity of Newtonian mechanics and of the Galilean transformation. Nevertheless, for ordinary experience with particles we ordinarily encounter (having masses greater than a microgram, dimensions greater than a micron, and speeds less than a megameter/sec) this formulation describes the world with sufficient precision.

The discrepancy between Newtonian mechanics and nature is remedied by a theory called *Quantum Mechanics* in the realm of small objects, and by the *Special Theory of Relativity* in the realm of high speeds. Both of these theories are so constructed that their predictions agree with those of Newtonian mechanics in the appropriate limit. And this is as it must be, for any physical theory must provide an accurate and concise description of experience, or it never finds acceptance. When new theories are born that seem to upset older ideas, their predictions must always be in agreement with the older ideas in the realm in which the older theories are already proven accurate. Such a view was first expressed by Niels Bohr (1885-1962) in 1923. Known as the *correspondence principle,* it may be stated as: *Different physical theories must yield convergent descriptions of the same phenomenon in their overlapping realms of validity*. For example, the *momentum* **p** of a particle of mass m moving with velocity **v** is given by relativity theory as

$$\mathbf{p} = m\gamma\mathbf{v}. \tag{3-1.1}$$

Prior to the special theory of relativity the momentum of a particle had been given by

$$\mathbf{p} = m\mathbf{v}. \tag{3-1.2}$$

Deductions from Eq. 3-1.2 had always been correct until the advent of radioactivity made it possible to perform experiments at speeds close to c. Then it was found that the relativistic form of the expression for momentum was in good agreement with experiment, while the nonrelativistic form of Eq. 3-1.2 was not. But in the nonrelativistic limit found by setting $c \to \infty$, we see that the two expressions agree, as required by the correspondence principle.

Some authors interpret Eqs. 3-1.1 and 3-1.2 to imply that momentum is always expressed as the product of mass by velocity, but that the mass m of a moving particle is different from its mass m_0 when it is at rest. This interpretation is summarized in the equations

$$\mathbf{p} = m\mathbf{v} \tag{3-1.3}$$

and

$$m = m_0\gamma = m_0/\sqrt{1 - v^2/c^2}. \tag{3-1.4}$$

Calculations resulting from Eqs. 3-1.3 are clearly identical with those arising from Eq. 3-1.1, and the choice of interpretation is one of taste. In this book no distinction will be made between rest mass and moving mass. The symbol m will always signify the mass determined when the particle is at rest in its inertial frame, such as by comparison with a standard mass through use of an inertial balance or a beam balance. Eq. 3-1.1 will always be used to describe the momentum in the relativistic case, with Eq. 3-1.2 as its nonrelativistic limit.

§3-2 Newton's Second Law   Newton's second law states: *If a net force acts on a body, the momentum of the body will be changed; the rate of change of the momentum is proportional to the net force and is in the direction of that force.*

The second law may be stated mathematically as

$$F = k\frac{d\mathbf{p}}{dt}, \tag{3-2.1}$$

where k is a scalar constant of proportionality. In the unit systems generally encountered in physics the constant k is defined as 1, a dimensionless constant, and Eq. 3-2.1 becomes

$$\mathbf{F} = \frac{d\mathbf{p}}{dt}. \tag{3-2.2}$$

In the nonrelativistic limit the momentum is given by Eq. 3-1.2 so that

$$\mathbf{F} = m\frac{d\mathbf{v}}{dt} = m\mathbf{a} \tag{3-2.3}$$

is the nonrelativistic form of Newton's second law.

At speeds comparable to c it is not possible to make the approximation that momentum is the product of mass times velocity. Instead we must use the correct relativistic form of the momentum as given in Eq. 3-1.1 and proceed from Newton's second law as given in Eq. 3-2.2. Repeating these equations for clarity, we have

$$\mathbf{F} = \frac{d\mathbf{p}}{dt}$$

and

$$\mathbf{p} = m\gamma\mathbf{v} = \frac{m\mathbf{v}}{\sqrt{1 - v^2/c^2}}.$$

Carrying out the indicated differentiation of $\mathbf{p}$ with respect to time t (which is measured in the laboratory frame), we find

$$\mathbf{F} = \frac{d}{dt} m\gamma\mathbf{v} = m\mathbf{v} \frac{d\gamma}{dt} + m\gamma \frac{d\mathbf{v}}{dt}. \qquad (3\text{-}2.4)$$

The first term of Eq. 3-2.4 is in the direction of the velocity vector. The second term contains the derivative of the velocity vector with respect to time. Since the change in the velocity vector may be in any direction, we may resolve that change into a component perpendicular to the velocity and a component parallel to the velocity. Writing the perpendicular component as the perpendicular component of the acceleration; that is, writing

$$\left(\frac{d\mathbf{v}}{dt}\right)_{\perp} = a_{\perp},$$

we find

$$F_{\perp} = m\gamma a_{\perp}. \qquad (3\text{-}2.5)$$

Before analyzing the component equation describing the component parallel to the velocity, let us consider the operations involved in computing $\frac{d\gamma}{dt}$. This will involve the computation of $\frac{dv^2}{dt}$. Now $v^2 = \mathbf{v} \cdot \mathbf{v}$, the scalar product of the vector $\mathbf{v}$ with itself. The scalar product of two vectors $\mathbf{A}$ and $\mathbf{B}$ is written as $\mathbf{A} \cdot \mathbf{B}$ and is equal to the product of the magnitude of the two vectors and the cosine of the angle between them; thus $\mathbf{A} \cdot \mathbf{B} = AB \cos \theta$. We must make use of a formula for the differentiation of the scalar product of two vectors, which is easily derived (Problem 3-2.1):

$$d(\mathbf{A} \cdot \mathbf{B}) = (d\mathbf{A}) \cdot \mathbf{B} + \mathbf{A} \cdot (d\mathbf{B}). \tag{3-2.6}$$

Thus $\qquad d(\mathbf{v} \cdot \mathbf{v}) = 2\mathbf{v} \cdot (d\mathbf{v}),$

and $\qquad \dfrac{dv^2}{dt} = 2\mathbf{v} \cdot \dfrac{d\mathbf{v}}{dt} = 2\mathbf{v} \cdot \mathbf{a}.$

If we write $\mathbf{a}$ as the vector sum of its components parallel to the velocity and perpendicular to the velocity, the scalar product $\mathbf{v} \cdot \mathbf{a}$ may be expressed as the product of the speed v by the parallel component of the acceleration $a_{\parallel}$, so that

$$\frac{dv^2}{dt} = 2va_{\parallel}. \tag{3-2.7}$$

Applying this result to Eq. 3-2.4, we have

$$F_{\parallel} = mv(-\tfrac{1}{2})(1 - v^2/c^2)^{-3/2}(-2va_{\parallel}/c^2) + m\gamma a_{\parallel}.$$

When we collect terms and clear fractions, the equation becomes

$$F_{\parallel} = m\gamma^3 a_{\parallel}. \tag{3-2.8a}$$

For comparison we repeat the equation for $F_{\perp}$,

$$F_{\perp} = m\gamma a_{\perp}. \tag{3-2.8b}$$

In Eqs. 3-2.8 the coefficients of a are sometimes given special names. Thus the coefficient of $a_{\parallel}$, $m\gamma^3$, is called the *longitudinal mass,* while the coefficient of $a_{\perp}$, $m\gamma$, is called the *transverse mass.*

The fact that the coefficients of the acceleration are different for the longitudinal and transverse component equations implies that *at high speeds the acceleration vector is not parallel to the force vector.*

Equation 3-2.8b, predicted by Einstein in 1905, was tested and confirmed by A. H. Bucherer in 1909, in an experiment in which β rays (electrons) emitted in radioactive decay were deflected by a magnetic field, where the force on a moving charged particle is always perpendicular to its direction of motion. Both Eqs. 3-2.8 have subsequently been confirmed many times, and their accuracy is now implicit in the design of charged particle accelerators.

3-2.1   The scalar product obeys the associative and distributive laws of arithmetic. Thus, for example, $(\mathbf{A} + \mathbf{B}) \cdot \mathbf{C} = \mathbf{A} \cdot \mathbf{C} + \mathbf{B} \cdot \mathbf{C}$. From the basic definition of a derivative as a differential quotient, show that $d(\mathbf{A} \cdot \mathbf{B}) = (d\mathbf{A}) \cdot \mathbf{B} + \mathbf{A} \cdot (d\mathbf{B})$.

§3-3 The Equivalence Principle   If we observe that an isolated object of mass m behaves as if it is experiencing a force $\mathbf{F}$ (say, because it causes a supporting spring to be deflected), then we find that we can make two possible statements about it. Either the object is in a gravitational field of field intensity $\mathbf{g}$ such that $\mathbf{F} = m\mathbf{g}$, or it is being accelerated (along with its supporting spring and the frame to which the spring is attached) with acceleration $\mathbf{a}$ such that $\mathbf{F} = m\mathbf{a}$ (in the low velocity limit). It is even possible that the object is experiencing some combination of gravitational field and accelerated motion, as in the case of a mass hanging from the ceiling of an elevator which is accelerating upward. But we cannot distinguish between the two causes. We cannot tell how much of the deflection of the spring is due to the acceleration of the elevator and how much is due to the gravitational field. In order to separate the two effects we would first have had to observe the deflection of the spring when the elevator was at rest, or when it was moving at constant speed in a straight line.

This observation, and similarly based experiments performed with great precision, have led to the concept that accelerated coordinate frames and gravitational fields are equivalent, a view summarized in the *equivalence principle,* which states that *it is impossible to distinguish between an accelerated coordinate frame and a gravitational field.* To quote Einstein, "This assumption of exact physical equivalence makes it impossible for us to speak of the absolute acceleration of the system of reference, just as the usual theory of relativity forbids us to talk of the absolute velocity of a system." The equivalence principle lies at the foundation of the general theory of relativity.

The special theory of relativity advises us that it is impossible for us to build an entirely self-contained speedometer that measures an absolute velocity. We must measure velocities with respect to some coordinate frame. We cannot have a velocimeter which is wholly built in, which makes no contact with an external frame of reference. In an automobile the speedometer measures motion with respect to the road; in an airplane the airspeed indicator measures speed with respect to the surrounding air mass; in a space ship the navigational instruments measure speed with respect to a planet or the sun.

In the same way the general theory of relativity and the equivalence principle advise us that it is impossible to build a wholly self-contained accelerometer. When accelerometers are used in inertial navigation, as in submarines and satellites, knowledge of the gravitational field must be supplied as independent input information, for the device itself cannot tell whether it is being accelerated, or is in a gravitational field, or both.

One interpretation of the word weight is the upward force exerted on an object by its supports. Thus we are "heavier" when we stand on the floor of an elevator which is accelerating upward, and we are "weightless" when the floor of the elevator is falling at the same acceleration as we would experience in free fall.

Let us consider the weight of a moving object. What is the weight of a puck which slides horizontally on a smooth floor at speed v? We interpret the word weight as meaning the force the floor exerts on the puck, and interpret the problem from the viewpoint of a set of observers on an inertial frame who see the equivalent problem, that of a puck sliding on the floor of an elevator which is accelerating upward in field free space. For this situation must be identical with the real one where the puck slides on the fixed floor in a uniform gravitational field. By Eq. 3-2.8b the inertial observers know that the floor must exert an upward force on the puck equal to $m\gamma g$, and they, as referees, declare that this is the weight of the moving puck. Thus we must conclude that a body moving horizontally in a uniform vertical gravitational field is heavier than it was at rest. If the weight of the body at rest is mg, then when it is moving horizontally with speed v, its weight is $m\gamma g = mg/\sqrt{1 - v^2/c^2}$.

§3-4 Transformation of Forces According to the Galilean transformation, the acceleration of a particle is the same as measured in either of two inertial frames. From Eq. 1-2.6 we have

$$\mathbf{a} = \mathbf{a}'.$$

If we multiply both sides of the equation by m, we find

$$m\mathbf{a} = m\mathbf{a}'.$$

Making use of the nonrelativistic form of Newton's second law in Eq. 3-2.3, we write for each of the two inertial frames that

$$\mathbf{F} = m\mathbf{a} \quad \text{and} \quad \mathbf{F}' = m\mathbf{a}'.$$

Thus we infer that the force acting on a particle is the same in both frames, that is,

$$\mathbf{F} = \mathbf{F}', \tag{3-4.1}$$

and we would conclude that the force acting on a particle is measured to have the same value in every inertial frame so long as the Galilean transformation is valid.

The situation is different at high speeds, where the Lorentz transformation is correct. The transformation equations for the acceleration are given by Eqs. 2-9.5 in the special case that the particle is instantaneously at rest in the primed frame. These equations are

$$\gamma^3 a_{||} = a'_{||} \quad \text{and} \quad \gamma^2 a_\perp = a'_\perp. \tag{3-4.2}$$

As before, we imply that the particle is instantaneously at rest in the primed frame but is accelerating with acceleration $\mathbf{a}'$ with respect to that frame, that the primed frame is moving with speed v in the $+x$ direction with respect to the unprimed or laboratory frame, and that observers in the laboratory frame measure the acceleration to be $\mathbf{a}$ with respect to the laboratory (unprimed) frame.

If we multiply each of Eqs. 3-4.2 by m, we find

$$m\gamma^3 a_{||} = ma'_{||} \qquad (3\text{-}4.3a)$$

and

$$m\gamma^2 a_{\perp} = ma'_{\perp}. \qquad (3\text{-}4.3b)$$

Let us now compare these results with Eqs. 3-2.8, which we write as

$$F_{||} = m\gamma^3 a_{||}$$

and

$$F_{\perp} = m\gamma a_{\perp}$$

when referring to the laboratory frame in which the particle is moving with speed v in the $+x$ direction, and as

$$F'_{||} = ma'_{||}$$

and

$$F'_{\perp} = ma'_{\perp}$$

when referring to the proper frame of the particle, in which the particle is instantaneously at rest, so that $\gamma' = 1$. Substituting these equations into Eq. 3-4.3, we find

$$F_{||} = F'_{||} \quad \text{and} \quad \gamma F_{\perp} = F'_{\perp}. \qquad (3\text{-}4.4)$$

The relativistic theory tells us that the forces on a particle are not the same when observed from different inertial frames, contrary to our intuition and to ordinary experience. But then, we have seen that we cannot infer what to expect at high velocities from our ordinary experience.

The distinctions that observers in different inertial frames must make in regard to the forces acting on rapidly moving particles play a very important role in our understanding of electricity and magnetism, and particularly in the interplay between electric and magnetic forces as observed in different frames.

Once again we note that in the nonrelativistic limit $c \to \infty$, we find $\gamma \to 1$, and the relativistic force transformation Eqs. 3-4.4 approach the nonrelativistic Eqs. 3-4.1.

3-4.1 The mass of the electron is 9.1×10^{-28} gm. (a) Find the acceleration of an electron in its proper frame (in which it is instantaneously at rest) if it is acted on by a force of $\mathbf{F}' = 9.1 \times 10^{-4} \, \mathbf{1}_z$ dynes. (b) What force does an observer in the laboratory frame believe to be acting on the electron, if he observes it to be moving at $v = 0.9998c \, \mathbf{1}_x$ with respect to the laboratory frame? (c) What acceleration does the laboratory observer compute the electron to have, by use of the relativistic relations between mass and acceleration? (d) What acceleration does the laboratory observer find for the electron if he translates the acceleration noted by the proper observer through use of the Lorentz transformation equations for acceleration? [(a) 10^{24} $1_{z'}$ cm/sec^2 (b) 1.8×10^{-5} 1_z dynes (c) 4×10^{20} 1_z cm/sec^2 (d) 4×10^{20} cm/sec^2]

3-4.2 The mass of a proton is 1.67×10^{-27} kgm. The proton experiences a force of $(1.67 \times 10^{-9}$ N$) \times (1_{x'} + 1_{z'})$ in its proper frame, in which it is instantaneously at rest. (a) Find the acceleration of the proton in this frame. (b) Find the angle between force and acceleration in this frame. As measured by a laboratory observer for whom the proton is moving with speed corresponding to $\beta = 0.98$ in the $+x$ direction, what is (c) the force on the proton, (d) the acceleration of the proton, and (e) the angle between the force and the acceleration? [(a) 10^{18} m/sec^2 $\times (1_{x'} + 1_{z'})$ (b) $0°$ (c) $1.67 \times 10^{-9}N \times (1_x + 0.2$ $1_z)$ (d) 10^{18} m/sec^2 $\times (1/125$ $1_x + 1/25$ 1_z (e) $67.4°$]

CHAPTER BIBLIOGRAPHY

A. Einstein, "On the Generalized Theory of Gravitation," Scientific American **182**, 13 (1950).

H. Bondi, "Relativity," Progress in Physics **22**, 97 (1959).

4 *Energy and Momentum*

§4.1 Work The concept of physical work as the result of the action of a force through a distance developed in mechanics and has had important repercussions in all of physics, as well as in other sciences. While the concept of work has physiological origins and is related to the feeling of tiredness, physical work is defined in such a way that tiredness is not a measure of work.

If a constant force $\mathbf{F}$ is moved through a displacement $\mathbf{s}$, we say that physical work W (a scalar) has been done, according to the equation

$$W = \mathbf{F} \cdot \mathbf{s} = Fs \cos \theta. \qquad (4\text{-}1.1)$$

The work is the product of the magnitude of the force times the magnitude of the displacement by the cosine of the angle between them (when they are drawn from a common origin). Alternatively, since the product $F \cos \theta$ is the component of the force parallel to the displacement, $F_{\parallel}$, we could rewrite Eq. 4-1.1 as

$$W = F_{\parallel} s. \qquad (4\text{-}1.2)$$

Note that no work is done by any force, however great, unless there is a displacement. No work is done by any force unless there is a component of the force in the direction of the displacement.

In the event that the force is variable we first express the work done when the force is moved through a small displacement $d\mathbf{s}$ as dW, so that

$$dW = \mathbf{F} \cdot d\mathbf{s}, \qquad (4\text{-}1.3)$$

and then integrate, to find the work done as the variable force traverses a particular path (see Fig. 4-1.1), so that

$$W = \int_{s_1}^{s_2} \mathbf{F} \cdot d\mathbf{s}. \qquad (4\text{-}1.4)$$

When work is done on an object, we find that there are changes in the speed with which it is moving, or in its shape, or in its temperature, or in its magnetization, or in some other physical

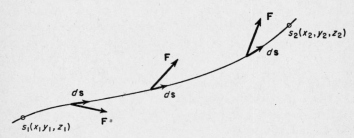

FIG. 4-1.1   If the force is different along different parts of the path, we must sum small increments of work, or must integrate, to find the work done in traversing the path from point s_1 to point s_2.

property. We sum up these observations by saying that the work done produces a change in the *energy* of the body. If the change is one of speed, we call the change one of *kinetic energy*. If the change is one of position or of configuration, we call the change one of *potential energy*. Changes in temperature are associated with *internal energy;* changes in magnetization are associated with *magnetic energy*.

Work and energy are measured in many different kinds of units. Since the concept is initially a mechanical one, the fundamental units of energy are based on its definition in mechanics. Thus we have the erg as the work done by a force of 1 dyne moving through a displacement of 1 cm. The joule is the work done by a force of 1 newton passing through a displacement of 1 meter. Other units of energy find wide use.

The *electron volt* is the energy acquired by an electron in passing through a potential difference of 1 volt. For our purposes it is sufficient to state that

$$1 \text{ electron volt} = 1.602 \times 10^{-12} \text{ erg} = 1.602 \times 10^{-19} \text{ joule}.$$

The calorie is the heat required to raise the temperature of 1 gram of water from 14.5 to 15.5°C. For our purposes it is sufficient to state that

$$1 \text{ calorie} = 4.185 \times 10^7 \text{ erg} = 4.185 \text{ joules.}$$

We will soon see that matter at rest in free space has energy in the form of mass, and that this energy, measured in units of mass, may be expressed in units of mechanical energy according to the equation

$$E = mc^2. \tag{4-1.5}$$

One atom of a substance whose atomic weight is 1 (1/12 the mass of a C^{12} atom) has a mass of $(6.025 \times 10^{23})^{-1}$ gm. The conversion of this mass unit to energy units is often expressed in million electron volts (MeV) as

$$1 \text{ atomic mass unit (amu)} = 931.5 \text{ MeV.}$$

§4.2 Kinetic Energy (Nonrelativistic)   If a force **F** acts on a particle of mass m through a displacement ds, the work done by the force on the particle is given by Eq. 4-1.3 as $dW = \mathbf{F} \cdot d\mathbf{s}$, and we must integrate the elements of work over the path of the particle to find the total work done on it, as indicated in §4-1.

In general the force is the rate of change of the momentum. In the nonrelativistic case this statement reduces to the form

$$\mathbf{F} = m \frac{d\mathbf{v}}{dt}.$$

When a particle moves with velocity **v**, the displacement ds that it experiences in a time dt may be expressed as

$$d\mathbf{s} = \mathbf{v} \, dt.$$

We may combine these statements in the definition of work as

$$dW = \mathbf{F} \cdot d\mathbf{s} = \left(m \frac{d\mathbf{v}}{dt} \right) \cdot (\mathbf{v} \, dt),$$

and canceling the dt which appears in both numerator and denominator, we find

$$dW = m \, (d\mathbf{v}) \cdot \mathbf{v}.$$

Integrating, we have

$$W = m \int \mathbf{v} \cdot d\mathbf{v}. \tag{4-2.1}$$

We have already seen that we may express v^2 as $\mathbf{v} \cdot \mathbf{v}$, so that

$$d(v^2) = d(\mathbf{v} \cdot \mathbf{v}) = \mathbf{v} \cdot d\mathbf{v} + d\mathbf{v} \cdot \mathbf{v} = 2\mathbf{v} \cdot d\mathbf{v}.$$

Substituting this result into Eq. 4-2.1, taking the initial velocity to be 0 and the final velocity to be $\mathbf{v}$, and inserting the limits of integration, we obtain

$$W = \int_0^v \frac{m}{2} d(v^2) = \frac{1}{2} mv^2.$$

We say that a particle acquires *kinetic energy* T equal to W as the result of the action of the force through a distance, and that the kinetic energy of the moving particle is given by the equation

$$T = \tfrac{1}{2}mv^2. \tag{4-2.2}$$

The kinetic energy may also be expressed in terms of the magnitude of the momentum; since in the nonrelativistic case $p = mv$, we have

$$T = \frac{p^2}{2m}. \tag{4-2.3}$$

§4-3 Kinetic Energy (Relativistic)   Recall that the definition of work in §4-1 did not depend in any way on the speed of the particle. Thus we may use the same procedure as before to find an expression for kinetic energy at high speeds. We repeat the initial steps of the development of §4-2, but at the appropriate place we must insert the relativistic expression for momentum instead of the nonrelativistic one. Thus we begin with

$$dW = \mathbf{F} \cdot d\mathbf{s}$$

and note that

$$d\mathbf{s} = \mathbf{v} \, dt,$$

but now we make use of the relativistic form of Newton's second law, which states that

$$\mathbf{F} = \frac{d\mathbf{p}}{dt} = \frac{dm\gamma\mathbf{v}}{dt}.$$

The work done in displacing the particle from rest at position 0 to a final velocity $\mathbf{v}$ at position s is given by

$$W = \int_0^s \mathbf{F} \cdot d\mathbf{s} = \int_0^s \left(\frac{dm\gamma\mathbf{v}}{dt}\right) \cdot (\mathbf{v}\, dt)$$

$$= \int_0^v [m\gamma\, (d\mathbf{v}) \cdot \mathbf{v} + (d\gamma)m\mathbf{v} \cdot \mathbf{v}].$$

Now

$$d\gamma = d(1 - v^2/c^2)^{-1/2} = (1 - v^2/c^2)^{-3/2}\, \mathbf{v} \cdot d\mathbf{v}\, c^{-2},$$

as we have seen. Using this result, and recalling that

$$\frac{\mathbf{v} \cdot d\mathbf{v}}{c^2} = \frac{1}{2}\, d\left(\frac{v^2}{c^2}\right),$$

we may substitute into the preceding equation for W to find

$$W = \frac{m}{2} \int_0^v \left(\frac{c^2}{(1 - v^2/c^2)^{1/2}} + \frac{v^2}{(1 - v^2/c^2)^{3/2}}\right) d\left(\frac{v^2}{c^2}\right),$$

which can be simplified to

$$W = \frac{mc^2}{2} \int_0^v \frac{d\left(\frac{v^2}{c^2}\right)}{(1 - v^2/c^2)^{3/2}}.$$

Performing the integration, we find

$$W = \left[\frac{mc^2}{(1 - v^2/c^2)^{1/2}}\right]_0^v.$$

When we substitute in the limits, we find the work done to be

$$W = m\gamma c^2 - mc^2. \qquad (4\text{-}3.1)$$

Since the second term on the right in Eq. 4-3.1 contains no velocity, we label the term *rest energy,* or mass energy, and say that an object of mass m has total energy E when it is moving with velocity $\mathbf{v}$, given by

$$E = m\gamma c^2. \qquad (4\text{-}3.2)$$

The difference between the total energy E and the rest energy mc^2 is the kinetic energy T. The kinetic energy T is the energy acquired by the particle as a result of the work done on it in raising its speed from 0 to v.

Accordingly, the kinetic energy T of a particle of mass m moving with velocity $\mathbf{v}$ is given by the equation

$$T = E - mc^2 = mc^2(\gamma - 1). \tag{4-3.3}$$

In the limit of low velocities, where v is much less than c, we may expand γ as a series to find

$$\gamma = (1 - v^2/c^2)^{-1/2} = 1 + \tfrac{1}{2}(v^2/c^2) \ldots \tag{4-3.4}$$

so that

$$T = mc^2(1 + \tfrac{1}{2}(v^2/c^2) \ldots - 1) = \tfrac{1}{2}mv^2.$$

As demanded by the correspondence principle, our two expressions for kinetic energy agree in the limit of low velocities.

To find a relation between energy and momentum we note that

$$E = m\gamma c^2 \quad \text{and} \quad \mathbf{p} = m\gamma \mathbf{v},$$

so that

$$E^2 - p^2c^2 = m^2\gamma^2c^4(1 - v^2/c^2) = m^2c^4,$$

or

$$E^2 = p^2c^2 + m^2c^4. \tag{4-3.5}$$

In Eq. 4-3.5, E and mc^2 are often expressed in MeV, so that a convenient unit of momentum is MeV/c. Incidentally, Eq. 4-3.5 is often remembered through the analogue of a right triangle, in which E is the hypotenuse.

It is remarkable that the relativistic relationship between energy and momentum is valid for all particles—even those of zero mass, like neutrinos or photons.

Electromagnetic radiation (light, radio, γ rays) can be described as a wave motion or as a particle motion. The wave description utilizes such terms as wavelength λ, say, the distance between two successive crests of the wave, and the frequency v, the number of vibrations per second. These quantities are related by the equation

$$\lambda v = c, \tag{4-3.6}$$

all quantities being measured in vacuum. The particle description speaks of electromagnetic radiation as made up of photons which have discrete amounts of energy. The two descriptions are related through the equation

$$E = h\nu, \qquad (4\text{-}3.7)$$

which gives the energy of a single photon of radiation whose wave description assigns to it a frequency ν. Photons of light have zero mass. Nevertheless the relation between their energy and their momentum is given by Eq. 4-3.5, for the momentum of a photon, p, is given by

$$p = \frac{h\nu}{c} = \frac{h}{\lambda}. \qquad (4\text{-}3.8)$$

The direction of the momentum of the photon is identified with the direction in which the wave is propagated.

In Eqs. 4-3.7 and 4-3.8 the symbol h represents a fundamental physical constant called *Planck's constant,* after its discoverer, Max Planck (1858-1947), which has the value

$$h = 6.625 \times 10^{-27} \text{ erg sec.}$$

Equation 4-3.8 was applied to the behavior of particles by Louis de Broglie (b. 1892) to yield a wavelength to be associated with moving particles, as

$$\lambda = h/p, \qquad (4\text{-}3.9)$$

an equation which is now known as the *de Broglie equation.*

The constant h determines the realm in which classical mechanics must blend into quantum mechanics, just as the constant c determines when classical mechanics must blend into relativity. The very small numerical value of h implies that particles of ordinary experience will demand an almost infinitesimally short wavelength to describe their motion, so short as to be undetectable, as for a child's marble whose mass is about 1 gm which is moving at a speed of a micron per second. These wave properties are displayed for particles whose mass is of the order of that of a proton or less. Again, the wave picture of light is to be modified according to the size of h, for this numerical value determines whether there is detectable energy in a single photon, or whether there is detectable momentum in a single photon. If a single photon cannot be detected, we should never arrive at a particle conception for light.

§4-4 Conservation of Linear Momentum If a single particle has no force acting on it, there will be no change in its momentum. We would therefore say that *the momentum of a single particle is constant if there is no external force acting on it,* and following the discussion of §3-2, this statement is independent of the speed of the particle.

Suppose that we have a system of particles, $m_1, m_2 \ldots m_n$,

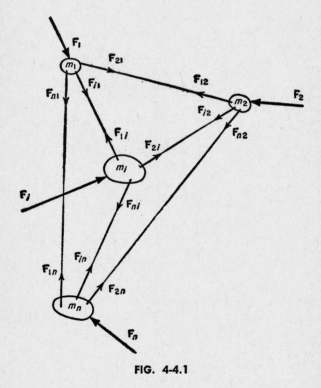

FIG. 4-4.1

which act on each other, and experience forces from sources outside the collection as well, as in Fig. 4-4.1. We will call the forces which the particles exert on each other *internal forces,* and forces which arise from outside the collection will be called *external forces.* Let us further suppose that the forces which the particles of the system exert on one another are equal and opposite, in conformity with the concept of the equality of action and reaction which is called *Newton's Third Law.* We use a double subscript notation to represent internal forces and a single subscript notation to represent external forces. Thus, $\mathbf{F}_{ij}$ *means the force exerted by particle i on particle j, while* $\mathbf{F}_i$ *means the net external force on particle i.* We apply Newton's second law to each of the particles of the collection, in turn, as

$$\mathbf{F}_1 + \mathbf{F}_{21} \ldots + \mathbf{F}_{i1} \ldots + \mathbf{F}_{n1} \quad = \frac{d\mathbf{p}_1}{dt},$$

$$\cdot$$
$$\cdot$$
$$\cdot$$

$$\mathbf{F}_i + \mathbf{F}_{1i} \ldots \ldots \ldots \ldots + \mathbf{F}_{ni} \quad = \frac{d\mathbf{p}_i}{dt},$$

$$\cdot$$
$$\cdot$$
$$\cdot$$

$$\mathbf{F}_n + \mathbf{F}_{1n} \ldots + \mathbf{F}_{in} \ldots + \mathbf{F}_{n-1,n} = \frac{d\mathbf{p}_n}{dt}.$$

Let us add these equations, making note of the fact that $\mathbf{F}_{ij} = -\mathbf{F}_{ji}$, so that the sum of the internal forces is zero, to find that

$$\mathbf{F}_1 + \mathbf{F}_2 \ldots + \mathbf{F}_i \ldots + \mathbf{F}_n = \frac{d}{dt}(\mathbf{p}_1 + \mathbf{p}_2 \ldots + \mathbf{p}_i \ldots + \mathbf{p}_n).$$

Thus the vector sum of the external forces acting on a collection of particles is equal to the rate of change of the total linear momentum of the collection.

If we write

$$\mathbf{F} = \sum_i \mathbf{F}_i \quad \text{and} \quad \mathbf{P} = \sum_i \mathbf{p}_i,$$

then
$$\mathbf{F} = \frac{d\mathbf{P}}{dt}. \tag{4-4.1}$$

In the special case that $\mathbf{F} = 0$ we see that $\mathbf{P}$ is constant. Thus, *if a system of particles is acted on by zero net external force, the total linear momentum of the system is constant.* This statement is called the law of *conservation of linear momentum.*

The law of conservation of linear momentum has been studied for systems ranging in size from nuclear to astronomical, in collisions between protons, between protons and electrons, and in everyday experience. No case of its violation has ever been detected.

The concept of a closed system, with the associated ability to ignore internal forces in dealing with momentum conservation, gives this concept great applicability.

We may consider the oars of a rowboat and the occupants and the water around it all part of a system. If the entire system is initially at rest, its total momentum must remain zero regardless of the manner in which the occupants manipulate the oars. The oars scoop small volumes of water backward, and the boat acquires equal forward momentum. Similarly, an airplane acquires forward momentum by giving air backward momentum, through the agency of a propeller or a jet engine. A jet airplane has readily available mass in the surrounding air which it can eject backward, but a rocket ship in outer space must carry along all the mass which it subsequently ejects as momentum. If a rocket ship is initially at rest in outer space, the total linear momentum of the rocket, its exhaust gases, and all its parts must forever be zero, so long as the rocket ship is acted on by no external forces.

The law of conservation of linear momentum is today regarded as having universal validity, independent of its derivation from Newton's laws of motion, though we have here based our discussion on these laws. Any proper formulation of physics must yield the result that momentum is conserved in closed systems (which experience no external force), for all deductions which have been made from the momentum conservation law have found experimental verification, and all pertinent experiments have been explained by it.

The neutrino was postulated by W. Pauli (1900-1958) in 1931 as a particle of zero charge which could conserve missing energy and angular momentum (spin) in β decay. By 1950 experiment had shown that the postulated particle could also account for the missing linear momentum in β decay. A decade later the neutrino was detected and its inferred properties verified.

In the preceding development the assertion that $\mathbf{F}_{ij} = -\mathbf{F}_{ji}$ implies that the forces between particles are propagated with infinite speed. To apply this development to the relativistic case, where the finite speed of propagation of the force fields must be taken into account, it is customary to attribute momentum to the field. In this way we arrive at the concept of the momentum in the electromagnetic field in classical electrodynamics. In 1901 the momentum of electromagnetic waves was verified experimentally by Nichols and Hull, in an experiment which showed that light exerted a force on a surface on which it fell, in quantitative agreement with the momentum conservation principle. Today, quantum electrodynamics speaks of electromagnetic radiation as being propagated by photons which have both energy and momentum, as we will see in our discussion of the Compton effect, in §5-2.

4-4.1 A positive pion $(\pi+)$ at rest decays to a positive muon $(\mu+)$ and a neutrino (v). The kinetic energy of the muon has been measured to be $T_\mu = 4.1$ MeV. The mass of the muon is known from other experiments to be 105.7 MeV. Find the mass of the pion. Do this nonrelativistically, and then repeat your calculation relativistically. The accepted mass of the pion is 139.6 MeV.

§4-5 Center of Mass (Nonrelativistic)   It is convenient to define the position vector of the center of mass $\mathbf{R}$ of a collection of particles by the equation

$$M\mathbf{R} = \sum_i m_i \mathbf{r}_i, \qquad (4\text{-}5.1)$$

where
$$M = \sum_i m_i$$

is the total mass of the collection of particles. By differentiating both sides of Eq. 4-5.1 and noting that

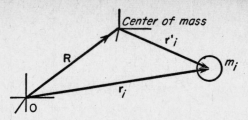

FIG. 4-5.1

$$\frac{d\mathbf{R}}{dt} = \mathbf{V} \quad \text{and} \quad \frac{d\mathbf{r}_i}{dt} = \mathbf{v}_i,$$

we find

$$\mathbf{P} = M\mathbf{V} = \sum_i m_i\mathbf{v}_i = \sum_i \mathbf{p}_i \qquad (4\text{-}5.2)$$

Eq. 4-5.2 tells us that the total momentum of the collection of particles is the same as the momentum of an imaginary particle whose mass is the mass of the entire collection, which moves with the center of mass.

Comparing Eq. 4-5.2 with Eq. 4-4.1, we see that the center of mass of a collection of particles moves in response to the total force on the collection just as a single particle would, for we have

$$\mathbf{F} = \frac{d\mathbf{P}}{dt}. \qquad (4\text{-}5.3)$$

If a shrapnel shell bursts in mid-air, the bits of shrapnel fly about under the influence of internal forces from the explosive, but the center of mass of the collection of particles continues on as a projectile, as though the shell never did burst. Of course, the aerodynamic forces on the explosive gases and the shell fragments are different than before, so that the trajectory of the center of mass is modified from what it would have been if there were no explosion.

If a rocket ship could be suspended in outer space and its engines were then started, the center of mass of the particles which were initially part of the ship would remain at rest forever, so long as no external forces act on any parts of the ship.

It is useful to consider the energy of a collection of particles in relation to the center of mass. Suppose that the position vector of the center of mass is $\mathbf{R}$ and the position vector of the i'th particle is $\mathbf{r}_i$, when measured from an arbitrary origin, but the position vector of the i'th particle is $\mathbf{r}'_i$ when measured from an origin at the center of mass, as shown in Fig. 4-5.1. We have

$$\mathbf{r}_i = \mathbf{R} + \mathbf{r}'_i. \tag{4-5.4}$$

Differentiating this equation with respect to t, we find

$$\mathbf{v}_i = \mathbf{V} + \mathbf{v}'_i.$$

The kinetic energy of the i'th particle is

$$T_i = \tfrac{1}{2}m_i v_i{}^2 = \tfrac{1}{2}m_i V^2 + \tfrac{1}{2}m_i v'{}_i{}^2 + m_i \mathbf{v}'_i \cdot \mathbf{V},$$

as measured in the laboratory frame.

Let us add together the kinetic energy of all the particles of the system to get the total kinetic energy T of the entire system. We find

$$T = \sum_i T_i = \tfrac{1}{2}\left(\sum_i m_i\right)V^2 + \sum_i \tfrac{1}{2}m_i v'{}_i{}^2 + \left[\frac{d}{dt}\left(\sum m_i \mathbf{r}'_i\right)\right] \cdot \mathbf{V}.$$

The bracketed part of the last term on the right is zero, for, from Eq. 4-5.1, the part of this term in parentheses serves to define the position of the center of mass in the primed frame, in which the center of mass is at the origin, and has position vector zero. We conclude that the last term on the right is zero and that the total kinetic energy of the system is

$$T = \tfrac{1}{2}MV^2 + \sum_i T'_i. \tag{4-5.5}$$

As stated by Eq. 4-5.5, *the total kinetic energy of a collection of particles about an arbitrary origin is equal to the kinetic energy of its center of mass plus the kinetic energy of the collection with respect to the center of mass.*

In the absence of external forces the momentum of the center of mass is constant, and so therefore must the energy of the center of mass be constant. The kinetic energy contained in the motion about the center of mass may vary; that is, the mechanical motion about the center of mass need not be conserved as mechanical kinetic energy.

We call the kinetic energy about the center of mass the *internal kinetic energy* of the collection. The internal kinetic energy of an ideal gas is characterized by its temperature. For one mole of ideal gas the total internal kinetic energy is given by $T = \frac{3}{2} R\theta$, where R is the universal gas constant and θ is the temperature in degrees Kelvin. We know that the temperature of a real gas may change even though no external forces act on it, as the gas expands and some of the internal kinetic energy is exchanged for internal potential energy, as in the case of an expanding refrigerant.

We say that the collisions between particles are *perfectly elastic* when the internal kinetic energy of the particles (about their center of mass) is the same before the collision as immediately after. We say that the collisions between particles are inelastic when the internal kinetic energy is not conserved. When two cars or two lumps of putty collide, some of the internal kinetic energy may go into deforming the objects, doing work against the forces which hold the body together. A collision is said to be *perfectly inelastic* if the bodies move along together with the same velocity after the collision, as in the case of two balls of putty; that is, the internal kinetic energy is zero after the collision if the collision is perfectly inelastic. The collision between two atoms is inelastic if one or both of the atoms is raised to an *excited state* from which it may subsequently radiate light. Thus we are sure that the atoms in a neon sign are making inelastic collisions, for otherwise they would not glow.

In all cases, regardless of whether the collisions are elastic or inelastic, the momentum and energy of the center of mass are conserved. For this reason physicists often consider collision processes in the *center of mass frame,* the frame in which the center of mass is at rest, for in this frame the total momentum of the system of particles is zero, and only the internal kinetic energy of the system need be considered.

To discuss the motion of a collection of particles in the center of mass frame we would first find the velocity of the center of mass from Eq. 4-5.2. We would then apply the Galilean transformation to find the motion of each of the particles of the system in the center of mass frame, and from this we would find the momentum and the kinetic energy of each of the particles in this frame.

4-5.1 A uniform cylinder 8 ft long which weighs 32 lb is subdivided by a thin internal partition into halves each 4 ft long. The left side A contains 32 lb of compressed gas, while the right side B is evacuated. The cylinder rests on its side on a smooth horizontal table. The partition bursts. When the gas has come to equilibrium inside the cylinder, (a) what distance has the cylinder been displaced, and (b) with what velocity is it moving? [(a) 1 ft (b) 0]

4-5.2 Prove that in an elastic collision between two identical bodies, one of which is initially at rest, the angle between their velocities after collision is $\pi/2$, except for the case of central impact. Do this two ways. Work the problem entirely in the laboratory frame; then work in the center of mass frame and translate the result to the laboratory frame. (Nonrelativistic case only)

4-5.3 The energy levels of a hydrogen atom permit it to absorb 10.2 eV of energy as internal energy. (a) What is the smallest kinetic energy a hydrogen atom must have in order that it may collide inelastically with a second hydrogen atom at rest? (b) What is the smallest energy an electron may have in order that it may collide inelastically with a hydrogen atom at rest? [(a) 20.4 eV (b) 10.2 eV]

4-5.4 Two identical cars collide head on in a perfectly inelastic collision. In case (a) one car is moving at speed v and the other car is at rest. In case (b) both cars are moving with the same speed v in opposite directions. Assuming that the damage done is directly proportional to the energy dissipated inelastically, how much more damage is done in case (b) than in case (a)? [4$\times$]

§**4-6 Transformation of Momentum and Energy (Relativistic)**
In the proper frame in which a particle is at rest its momentum is zero, and its energy is mc^2. Since the proper frame is moving with velocity **V** with respect to the laboratory, the momentum of the particle as measured in the laboratory frame is given by $p_x = m\gamma_0 V$, $p_{y,z} = 0$, and its energy is given by $E = m\gamma_0 c^2$, where $\gamma_0 = (1 - V^2/c^2)^{-1/2}$.

We might find transformation equations for momentum and

energy by applying the transformation equations for the velocity, Eqs. 2-5.2, to the equations for the momentum and energy. But it is more instructive to follow a different procedure.

Recall that the Lorentz transformation equations give time a role analogous to that of a position coordinate. For this reason we speak of relativity as being a four-dimensional study. A relativistic displacement vector must have four components, one for each dimension of the relativistic space, rather than simply three components corresponding to the three dimensions of ordinary space vectors. The relativistic displacement is the prototype for a vector quantity in relativity, just as the three-dimensional displacement is the prototype for a vector quantity in everyday experience. We will see that the fourth component of the momentum vector whose three space components constitute the momentum is E/c^2.

Recall that a light flash at the origin, at the instant the primed and unprimed origins coincide, spreads out as a sphere in both primed and unprimed frames, as in §2-1. The equation

$$x^2 + y^2 + z^2 = c^2t^2$$

describes the light sphere in the unprimed frame, and a similar equation describes it in the primed frame.

A photon on the light sphere has both energy and momentum, and since the photon is massless these are related, from Eq. 4-3.5, as

$$p_x{}^2 + p_y{}^2 + p_z{}^2 = E^2/c^2$$

in the unprimed frame, and by a similar equation in the primed frame.

For both sets of equations to be simultaneously true in all inertial frames, momentum and energy must transform in the same way as spatial displacement and time. Thus we may find the transformation equations for momentum and energy by replacing x by p_x, y by p_y, z by p_z, and t by E/c^2 in the Lorentz transformation equations, as given in Eqs. 2-1.3. Thus we have

$$p'_x = \gamma_0 \left(p_x - V \frac{E}{c^2} \right), \quad \text{and} \quad p_x = \gamma_0 \left(p'_x + V \frac{E'}{c^2} \right); \quad (4\text{-}6.1)$$

$$p'_{y,z} = p_{y,z}, \qquad\qquad\qquad p_{y,z} = p'_{y,z};$$

$$E' = \gamma_0(E - Vp_x), \qquad\qquad E = \gamma_0(E' + Vp'_x).$$

In these equations γ_0 relates to the motion of the frames in the usual way, for $\gamma_0{}^{-2} = 1 - V^2/c^2$. The velocity of the particle in the unprimed frame is **v**; its momentum in this frame is $\mathbf{p} = m\gamma\mathbf{v}$, where $\gamma^{-2} = 1 - v^2/c^2$. The velocity of the particle in the primed frame is **v'**; its momentum in the primed frame is $\mathbf{p'} = m\gamma'\mathbf{v'}$, where $\gamma'^{-2} = 1 - v'^2/c^2$.

If these equations are used to transform energy and momentum, then the relativistic relation between energy and momentum given in Eq. 4-3.5 as

$$E^2 = p^2c^2 + m^2c^4 \qquad\qquad (4\text{-}6.2)$$

is true for all particles in all inertial frames. Indeed, the transformation equations were derived on the assumption that this was so. We may verify that on substitution of Eq. 4-6.1 into Eq. 4-6.2 we achieve the equation

$$E'^2 = p'^2c^2 + m^2c^4. \qquad\qquad (4\text{-}6.3)$$

We say that Eq. 4-6.2 is *relativistically covariant,* for this equation retains the same form and the symbols retain the same meaning in all inertial frames.

Consider the relationship between the conservation of linear momentum and the conservation of energy. In nonrelativistic mechanics these are independent relationships. But in relativity the two conservation principles are really one, for momentum and energy are intimately related through the transformation equations of 4-6.1. Momentum and energy form a four-vector, just as do displacement and time. If the total momentum of a collection of particles is constant in every inertial frame, then the total energy of that collection is also constant in every inertial frame. This is the immediate implication of the transformation equations, 4-6.1. Thus if we say Σp_x is constant and $\Sigma p'_x$ is constant, then it follows that ΣE is constant and $\Sigma E'$ is constant, simply by summing the transformation equation for p_x for all of the particles of the collection.

4-6.1 Derive transformation equations for momentum and energy by applying Eqs. 2-5.2 to Eqs. 3-1.1 and 4-3.2.

4-6.2 Verify the transformation from Eq. 4-6.2 to 4-6.3.

4-6.3 Repeat problem 4-5.2 for the relativistic case.

4-6.4 Show that the speed of a particle is given by $v = dE/dp$.

4-6.5 Find the greatest angle through which a nonrelativistic α particle can be deflected by striking a stationary proton. [14°]

4-6.6 Prove that if kinetic energy is conserved in the collision between two bodies in one inertial frame, then it is conserved in every inertial frame. Note that momentum is always conserved in collisions, but that kinetic energy is only conserved in elastic collisions.

§4-7 Center of Mass (Relativistic)   Let us develop our arguments about the center of mass and the center of mass frame in a manner analogous to our development of these ideas in the non-relativistic case. Suppose we define the *center of mass frame* as the inertial frame in which the total momentum of the collection of particles is zero. But the procedure is somewhat more complicated at high speeds than it was in the nonrelativistic case.

We first find the total momentum of a collection of particles as observed in the laboratory frame. Let us choose the x direction as the direction of this momentum vector. Then the y and z components of the total momentum of the collection of particles are zero, as seen in the laboratory frame. From the transformation equations these components of the momentum are zero in all other inertial frames moving at constant speed in the x direction with respect to the laboratory frame.

The total x momentum, P'_x, in the center of mass frame is zero. It is given by

$$0 = P'_x = \sum_i (p'_x)_i = \gamma_0 \left[\sum_i (p_x)_i - \frac{V}{c^2} \sum_i E_i \right],$$

from the transformation equation for p'_x in Eqs. 4-6.1. Writing **P** for the total momentum of the collection in the laboratory frame, and E for the total energy in the laboratory frame, we note that

$$\sum_i (p_x)_i = P \quad \text{and} \quad \sum_i E_i = E.$$

Solving the preceding equation, we find

$$\mathbf{V} = \frac{c^2}{E} \mathbf{P}. \tag{4-7.1}$$

In Eq. 4-7.1 we have written the result in vector form, for the directions of both quantities are evidently the x direction, but we no longer need to preserve the manner in which we set up the coordinate frame. The center of mass frame is moving with velocity **V** with respect to the laboratory frame, as given by Eq. 4-7.1.

As in the nonrelativistic case, we imagine that there is a particle of mass M located at the center of mass. As observed in the laboratory frame, the momentum of this particle would be set equal to the total momentum of the particles of the collection. Thus we have

$$\mathbf{P} = M\gamma_0\mathbf{V}, \tag{4-7.2}$$

so that the mass of the imaginary particle is obtained by substituting Eq. 4-7.2 into Eq. 4-7.1, as

$$\mathbf{V} = \frac{c^2}{E} M\gamma_0\mathbf{V},$$

or

$$M = \frac{E}{\gamma_0 c^2}. \tag{4-7.3}$$

The mass of the equivalent particle is not simply the sum of the masses of the particles of the collection, but the energy of the equivalent particle in the laboratory frame is equal to the total energy of the collection in the laboratory frame. The equivalent particle has the same momentum as the total momentum of the collection and the same energy as the total energy of the collection.

In the center of mass frame the equivalent particle is at rest, so that Eq. 4-7.3 becomes

$$M = \frac{E}{c^2},\qquad(4\text{-}7.4)$$

where we now must interpret E as the total energy of the collection of particles in the center of mass frame.

The center of mass frame might be thought to be the proper frame of the collection of particles. Thus if a tank of gas is at rest in the laboratory, then the laboratory frame is the frame in which the center of mass of the collection is at rest, and is the proper frame for the gas and its container.

If energy is added to the collection of particles by any means whatever, then we find, from Eq. 4-7.4, that the equivalent mass of the collection is also changed according to

$$\Delta M = \frac{\Delta E}{c^2}.\qquad(4\text{-}7.5)$$

In the discussion which led to Eq. 4-7.5 we only considered the rest energy of individual particles and the energy due to their motion. Experiment has shown that all forms of energy—rest energy, kinetic energy, and potential energy—affect the equivalent mass of a collection of particles, and Eq. 4-7.5, which defines the conversion of mass to energy, is a completely general relationship. When a neutron and proton form a stable configuration of negative potential energy called a deuteron, the mass of the collection is lower than the summed masses of the separate particles by the amount of the negative potential energy. When a gas is heated, the molecules of gas acquire kinetic energy, and the mass of the collection is increased.

The conclusion of Eq. 4-7.5, that energy may be given to a system thereby increasing its mass, or that energy may be taken from a system thereby decreasing its mass, has now been verified by many different experiments.

A system consisting of two particles, an electron and a positron, may give up all of its mass in an annihilation process in which two photons are created.

A system consisting of many protons and neutrons (the nucleus of an atom) may alter its configuration and form subsystems (fission fragments). The mass of the fragments is less than the mass of the parent. To conserve energy the fission fragments must acquire kinetic energy equivalent to the mass difference. This is the internal kinetic energy (energy about the center of mass) which appears as "heat" in nuclear reactors or in atomic bombs.

As we have here defined mass, there can be no mass change of a fundamental particle, for the mass of a particle is to be determined when that particle is at rest, as in a beam balance, or in an inertial balance. The mass of a system of particles may be altered when that system gains or loses energy. In addition, the kinetic energy of a rapidly moving particle may be converted to radiation, or may impart mass to a system, as in the creation of pions by rapidly moving protons. In all cases which involve measurable mass changes Eq. 4-7.5 has been verified quantitatively.

4-7.1 Neutrons of 3 MeV kinetic energy are scattered by protons. Find the kinetic energy of the recoil protons at (a) $0°$ and (b) $45°$. Angles are measured relative to the initial direction of the neutron. [(a) 3 MeV (b) 1.5 MeV]

4-7.2 Radium disintegrates into radon by the emission of an α particle. Find the kinetic energy of (a) the α particle and (b) the recoil nucleus. Atomic masses are: radium 226.10309 amu; radon 222.09397 amu; helium 4.00388 amu. [(a) 4.80 MeV (b) 0.08 MeV]

4-7.3 Show that the recoil energy of a nucleus of mass M is $h\nu/2Mc^2$ times the energy of an emitted photon. Find the recoil energy of a Cs^{137} nucleus when a γ ray of 662 KeV is emitted. [1.70 eV]

4-7.4 Is it possible for a photon to interact with an electron at rest and give all of its energy to the electron as kinetic energy?

4-7.5 What fraction of the energy of a rapidly moving proton is not available for inelastic interactions in proton-proton collisions when the target proton is at rest in the laboratory and the energy of the accelerator is (a) 3 GeV (b) 7 GeV (c) 25 GeV (d) 200 GeV (e) 1000 GeV? REF.: G. K. O'Neil, Science **141**, 679 (1963). [(a) 0.6 (b) 0.72 (c) 0.8 (d) 0.92 (e) 0.96]

4-7.6 If a proton accelerator were designed with two storage rings in which two beams of the same energy could be directed toward each other, all of the kinetic energy with respect to the laboratory would be available for inelastic collisions, for the laboratory is the center of mass frame. What energy would be required of a stationary target machine to produce the same available interaction energy as a colliding pair of stored beams with an energy of (a) 3 GeV (b) 25 GeV (c) 31 GeV? REF.: G. K. O'Neil, Science **141,** 679 (1963). [(a) 31 GeV (b) 1360 GeV (c) 2040 GeV]

4-7.7 A chemical balance customarily weighs to a sensitivity of about 0.1 mg. How much energy in ergs would be liberated in a chemical reaction if the change in mass were detectable in a weighing? [9×10^{16} ergs]

4-7.8 The energy required to ionize a helium atom is 24.6 eV. If helium gas is bombarded with charged particles, at what incident energy will ionization of helium just be observed if the projectiles are (a) α particles (b) protons (c) electrons? [(a) 49.2 eV (b) 30.8 eV (c) 24.6 eV]

CHAPTER BIBLIOGRAPHY

W. Bertozzi, *The Ultimate Speed, An exploration with high energy electrons* (a film), Educational Services Inc., Watertown, Mass.

W. Bertozzi, "Speed and Kinetic Energy of Relativistic Electrons," Am. J. Phys. **32,** 551 (1964).

P. Morrison, "The Neutrino," Scientific American **194,** 59 (1956).

R. E. Pollock, "Resonant Detection of Light Pressure by a Torsion Pendulum in Air—An Experiment for Underclass Laboratories," Am. J. Phys. **31,** 901 (1963).

F. Reines and C. L. Cowan, Jr., "The Neutrino," Nature **178,** 446 (1956).

5 *Some Relativistic Phenomena*

§5-1 Pair Production and Annihilation If energy could be converted from one form to another without inhibition, we might wonder how any sort of stability might be achieved in the universe. Clearly there must be some restraint on the free interchange of energy. In the formulation of physics such restraints often take the form of conservation principles. One of these is the law of *conservation of charge,* which states that *the total electric charge content of the universe must remain constant.* Thus a single electron cannot vanish, giving its energy to photons. But a positron is a positively charged particle, identical in every other way to the electron. An electron-positron pair may vanish or be created without violating the charge conservation principle.

The mass of an electron, expressed in energy units, is 0.5108 MeV. An electron-positron pair at rest in the laboratory may annihilate with the emission of a pair of photons of equal energy which move in opposite directions, so as to conserve linear momentum. The energy of each photon is given by the expression

$$h\nu = mc^2 = 0.5108 \text{ MeV}. \tag{5-1.1}$$

Thus the wavelength of annihilation radiation is

$$\lambda = h/mc. \tag{5-1.2}$$

Note that the electron and positron are themselves stable particles.

Positrons are emitted in the radioactive decay of some artificially radioactive nuclei, such as in the reaction $_{29}\text{Cu}^{64} \rightarrow _{28}\text{Ni}^{64} + \beta^+$. When positrons from such a source impinge on a place where there are many electrons, as in a block of copper, they rapidly come to rest. The range of these positrons in copper is about 300μ. On measurement we find that monochromatic annihilation radiation is produced whose wavelength is 0.2426×10^{-9} cm. Other experiments have shown that two photons are emitted simultaneously in opposite directions.

In studying the inverse process we find that a single photon cannot materialize an electron-positron pair in free space, regardless of its energy. Energy conservation alone is not enough. Momentum needs to be conserved also, and momentum could not be conserved in such a process. We may easily see this by considering the process of pair production in the center of mass frame of the newly created electron-positron pair. The momentum of the pair is zero in this frame, but since the velocity of light is c in every frame, the momentum of the photon cannot be zero.

Momentum conservation forbids pair production in free space, but pair production can take place in the neighborhood of a

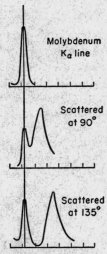

Molybdenum
K_a line

Scattered
at 90°

Scattered
at 135°

FIG. 5-2.1   Wavelength alterations of the modified line in the Compton effect at 90° and 135°. The unmodified line is also shown [After A. H. Compton, Am. J. Phys. 29, 817 (1961)].

third particle whose recoil can conserve momentum. Pair production commonly takes place in the field of a nucleus. The very large mass of a nucleus enables it to conserve momentum though moving at low speeds, so that the energy it requires is below the limit of measurement.

To conserve energy the pair production process cannot take place at photon energies less than the mass of the particles. We

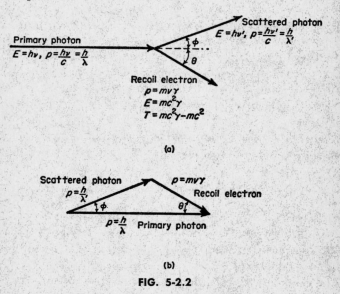

(a)

(b)

FIG. 5-2.2

observe that the threshold energy for pair production is 1.02 MeV, in agreement with conservation principles.

§5-2 Compton Effect In 1922 A. H. Compton (1892-1962) utilized the concept of an elastic collision between a photon and an electron to explain his observations of the scattering of x-rays. Compton found that x-rays scattered from a block of graphite were not all of the same wavelength as the incident radiation, as shown in Fig. 5-2.1. We apply the momentum conservation conditions, using the notation of Fig. 5-2.2 but taking E and p as the energy and momentum of the recoil electron, to obtain

$$p^2 = \frac{h^2}{\lambda'^2} + \frac{h^2}{\lambda^2} - \frac{2h^2}{\lambda\lambda'} \cos \phi \qquad (5\text{-}2.1)$$

or

$$p^2c^2 = \frac{h^2c^2}{\lambda'^2\lambda^2} (\lambda^2 + \lambda'^2 - 2\lambda\lambda' \cos \phi). \qquad (5\text{-}2.2)$$

The energy conservation condition yields

$$E = \frac{hc}{\lambda} - \frac{hc}{\lambda'} + mc^2, \qquad (5\text{-}2.3)$$

or

$$E = \frac{hc}{\lambda'\lambda} (\lambda' - \lambda) + mc^2, \qquad (5\text{-}2.4)$$

which may be squared to give

$$E^2 = \frac{h^2c^2}{\lambda'^2\lambda^2} (\lambda'^2 + \lambda^2) - \frac{2h^2c^2}{\lambda'\lambda} + \frac{2hmc^3(\lambda' - \lambda)}{\lambda'\lambda} + m^2c^4.$$

Making use of the relativistic relation between energy and momentum, Eq. 4-3.5, we find that

$$\lambda' - \lambda = \frac{h}{mc} (1 - \cos \phi). \qquad (5\text{-}2.5)$$

The quantity $h/mc = 0.02426 \times 10^{-8}$ cm is known as the *Compton wavelength,* for all photons scattered through $\pi/2$ have at least this wavelength. It is also the wavelength of annihilation radiation, Eq. 5-1.2.

The Compton effect is the fundamental process through which electromagnetic radiation is elastically scattered by matter. The radiation interacts with electrons in this scattering process. When the recoil energy of the electron is sufficiently great that the electron is disengaged from the parent atom or the parent lattice, then the electron is free, and a shift of wavelength of the scattered radiation occurs. But even at relatively high x-ray energies the recoil momentum is taken up by the entire atom or the entire lattice a significant part of the time. For this reason the scattered radiation is sometimes unaltered in wavelength, since a heavy atom or a lattice can absorb an appreciable amount of momentum without acquiring significant kinetic energy. When light or radio waves are scattered by matter, the recoil energy of the electron is so small that we must think of it as bound. The recoil momentum is always absorbed by the parent atom or lattice, and there is no detectable shift in wavelength in elastic scattering processes at low energy.

At low energy an appropriate analysis may be made by considering that the effect of the passing electromagnetic wave on an electron is through its oscillating electric field. The electron vibrates at the frequency of the driving field, and radiates energy as a result of its acceleration. The radiated energy is of the same frequency as the incident field. This approach to the scattering problem was made by J. J. Thomson and is known as *Thomson scattering,* a form of analysis which may be regarded as the low-energy limit of the Compton effect.

5-2.1 Determine the change in wavelength produced when an x-ray photon is scattered by an electron through an angle of (a) 90° (b) 180°. [(a) 0.242×10^{-8} cm (b) 0.0484×10^{-8} cm]

5-2.2 X-rays of wavelength 0.5×10^{-8} cm are scattered by free electrons in a block of carbon, through 90°. Find the momentum of the (a) incident photons, (b) scattered photons, (c) recoil electrons, and (d) the energy of the recoil electrons. [(a) 1.32×10^{-18} gm cm/sec (b) 1.26×10^{-18} gm cm/sec (c) 1.82×10^{-18} gm cm/sec (d) 1.92×10^{-9} erg]

§5-3 Threshold for π_0 Meson Production In the inelastic collisions encountered in high-energy physics, new particles are produced by the conversion of internal kinetic energy into matter. Because of the requirements of the law of conservation of momentum, a bombarding particle must have considerably more kinetic energy in the laboratory frame than is superficially implied by the mass of the newly manufactured particle. This is because the momentum and energy of the center of mass must be conserved. Only the internal energy in a collision may be converted into matter; this is the kinetic energy of the particles in the center of mass frame.

Let us consider the energy threshold for the production of uncharged π_0 mesons, whose mass is 264.4 times the mass of an electron, in the collisions of protons on protons. The reaction may be described symbolically as

$$p + p \rightarrow p + p + \pi_0.$$

In the center of mass frame all of the product particles will be at rest at threshold; that is, they will have no internal kinetic energy—the collision is perfectly inelastic, with all the kinetic energy being converted to another form.

In the laboratory frame the particles will all be moving with the same velocity V as the center of mass at threshold. To find V we note that before the collision only the proton from the accelerator is moving. The proton of the target, say liquid hydrogen, is at rest. The total energy E and momentum p before collision are

$$E = m_p c^2 \gamma + m_p c^2 = m_p c^2 (\gamma + 1)$$

and

$$\mathbf{p} = m_p \gamma \mathbf{v},$$

where

$$\gamma^{-2} = 1 - v^2/c^2.$$

From Eq. 4-7.1 the velocity V of the center of mass is given by

$$\mathbf{V} = \frac{c^2}{E} \mathbf{P} = \frac{\gamma}{\gamma + 1} \mathbf{v}.$$

The center of mass motion (and the motion of the reaction products at threshold) is characterized by γ_0, where

$$\gamma_0^{-2} = 1 - V^2/c^2 = \frac{2}{1 + \gamma}.$$

The energy of the reaction products in the laboratory frame after the collision is given by

$$(E_{\text{lab}})_{\text{after}} = (2m_p + m_{\pi_0}) c^2 \gamma_0.$$

Equating the energy of the system in the laboratory frame before and after the collision, we find

$$m_p c^2 (\gamma + 1) = (2m_p + m_{\pi_0}) c^2 \left(\frac{1 + \gamma}{2} \right)^2.$$

Squaring both sides of the equation and clearing terms, we find

$$2(1 + \gamma) = (2 + m_{\pi_0}/m_p)^2,$$

or
$$\gamma = \tfrac{1}{2}(2 + m_{\pi_0}/m_p)^2 - 1.$$

By Eq. 4-3.3, the kinetic energy of the incident proton at this value of γ is

$$T = m_p c^2(\gamma - 1) = \frac{m_p c^2}{2}\left(4 + 4\frac{m_{\pi_0}}{m_p} + \frac{m_{\pi_0}^2}{m_p^2}\right) - 2m_p c^2.$$

Simplifying, we find

$$T = m_{\pi_0} c^2\left(2 + \frac{m_{\pi_0}}{2m_p}\right). \qquad (5\text{-}3.1)$$

Since $m_p = 1836\, m_e$ and $m_{\pi_0} = 264\, m_e$, we find that the threshold in kinetic energy at which an accelerated proton beam will begin to produce π_0 mesons in a hydrogen target will be $T = 2.24\, m_{\pi_0} c^2 = 301$ MeV. The energy required in the beam is close to $2\tfrac{1}{4}$ times the mass energy of the π_0 meson.

5.3.1 Find the threshold for (a) the reaction

$$\bar{p} + p \rightarrow \Lambda_0 + \bar{\Lambda}_0.$$

the neutral lambda (Λ_0) particle and its antiparticle each have a mass of 2182 m_e; (b) the production of a proton-antiproton ($\bar{p}$) pair in the reaction

$$p + p \rightarrow p + p + p + \bar{p},$$

where accelerated protons strike a hydrogen target and convert their kinetic energy into the proton-antiproton pair. [(a) 763 MeV (b) 5.6 GeV]

§5-4 Doppler Effect Again the universality of the Lorentz transformation equations may be illustrated by applying the relativistic momentum-energy transformation, Eqs. 4-6.1, to the behavior of a photon.

   Suppose a photon is observed in a frame in which the source of the light is at rest. We call this the primed frame. In the primed frame the frequency of the light is ν', and the light is observed to make an angle θ' with the x' axis. The momentum and energy of the photon may then be described by the equations

$$p'_x = \frac{h\nu'}{c} \cos \theta', \qquad (5\text{-}4.1)$$

$$p'_y = \frac{h\nu'}{c} \sin \theta',$$

$$p'_z = 0,$$

and
$$E' = h\nu'.$$

Let us find the momentum and energy of the photon as measured in the laboratory frame by use of Eqs. 4-6.1. In the laboratory frame the photon would be measured to have frequency ν and to be moving with an angle θ with respect to the x axis so that

$$p_x = \frac{h\nu}{c} \cos \theta = \gamma_0 \left(\frac{h\nu'}{c} \cos \theta' + V \frac{h\nu'}{c^2} \right), \qquad (5\text{-}4.2)$$

$$p_y = \frac{h\nu}{c} \sin \theta = \frac{h\nu'}{c} \sin \theta',$$

$$p_z = 0,$$

$$E = h\nu = \gamma_0 \left(h\nu' + V \frac{h\nu'}{c} \cos \theta' \right).$$

Simplifying these equations, we find

$$\nu \cos \theta = \gamma_0 \nu'(\cos \theta' + V/c), \qquad (5\text{-}4.3\text{a})$$
$$\nu \sin \theta = \nu' \sin \theta', \qquad (5\text{-}4.3\text{b})$$

and
$$\nu = \gamma_0 \nu' \left(1 + \frac{V}{c} \cos \theta' \right). \qquad (5\text{-}4.3\text{c})$$

If we divide Eq. 5-4.3a by 5-4.3c, we find

$$\cos \theta = \frac{\cos \theta' + V/c}{1 + (V/c) \cos \theta'}. \qquad (5\text{-}4.4)$$

We have encountered Eq. 5-4.4 before, in the relativistic expression for aberration, Eq. 2-7.3, which was derived from the velocity addition formulas.

We have achieved an additional result as well. Not only will a light ray be observed to travel in different directions in two different inertial frames, but the frequency of the light will be measured differently by observers in the two frames. In the proper frame of the source the light will have the same frequency when proper observers measure it, whatever their position. In the laboratory frame, however, the frequency will depend on the angle θ which the light makes with the direction in which its source is observed to move. This is known as the *Doppler effect*, originally discovered in sound, and interpreted as due to the motion of the source or the observer with respect to the medium through which the sound was transmitted, the air. Even though there is no preferred medium for the transmission of light through a vacuum, nevertheless we still find a relativistic Doppler effect, due to time dilation and to the Lorentz contraction.

If in the laboratory frame the light is seen from $\pi/2$ to the direction of motion, then $\theta = \pi/2$, and from Eq. 5-4.4, $\cos \theta' = -V/c$. Putting this result into Eq. 5-4.3c, we find that

$$\gamma_0 \nu = \nu'. \tag{5-4.5}$$

This is called the *transverse Doppler effect*, for the observation is transverse to the direction of motion.

If the light is observed in the direction of motion, then $\theta = 0$. From Eq. 5-4.4 we find $\theta' = 0$, and

$$\nu = \nu' \left(\frac{1 + V/c}{1 - V/c}\right)^{1/2}; \tag{5-4.6}$$

that is, the light is shifted to the blue. When $\theta' = \pi$, the plus and minus signs in Eq. 5-4.6 are interchanged, and the light is shifted to the red. This is known as the *longitudinal Doppler effect*.

By means of the longitudinal Doppler effect the speed of rotation of distant double stars may be determined, for when one star is approaching the earth the other is receding, and the spectral lines of light from hydrogen atoms in the star pair become measurably broadened as their frequency is Doppler shifted.

Even though isolated atoms emit light which is nearly monochromatic, the light from a hot gas of atoms will be more diffuse in frequency because of the Doppler shifts due to the motion of atoms toward and away from the spectrometer. This is known as the *Doppler broadening* of spectral lines.

5-4.1 The wavelength of the α line of hydrogen is 6561.01 A° (1A° = 10^{-8} cm). What will be the measured wavelength of the H_α line in the absorption spectrum of a receding star moving at 3×10^6 m/sec away from the earth? [6627A°]

5-4.2 Calculate the width of H_α lines due to Doppler broadening at 6000°K. Assume that the maximum speed with which hydrogen atoms approach or recede from the spectrometer is estimated from the kinetic theory of gases to be given by the equation $\frac{1}{2}mv^2 = \frac{3}{2}kT$ ($k = 1.38 \times 10^{-23}$ joule/molecule $-°K$). [0.3A°]

5-4.3 The H_α lines measured on earth from opposite ends of the sun's equator differ in wavelength by 0.091A°. If the solar diameter is 865,000 miles, find the period of the rotation of this material of the sun, assuming rotation to be the cause of the effect. [25 days]

5-4.4. An electron-positron pair annihilates in free space, emitting two photons, each of energy 0.5108 MeV, in opposite directions in the proper frame. If this frame moves at $V = 0.9c$ with respect to the laboratory, and if the photons are emitted at an angle ϕ with respect to **V**, find the angle made by each of the photons with **V** and the energy of each of the two photons as determined in the laboratory, for $\phi =$ (a) 0° (b) 37° (c) 53° (d) 90°. (e) If an apparatus is set up in the laboratory which is capable of detecting two photons of the same energy coming from different directions and of determining whether they were emitted simultaneously, for what photon energy (determined in the laboratory) should we expect to measure coincidences in the laboratory? [(a) 0°, 2.21 MeV; 180°, 0.12 MeV (b) 19°, 2.1 MeV; $-60°$, 0.24 MeV (c) 21°, 1.8 MeV; $-47°$, 0.46 MeV (d) 90°, 1.16 MeV; $-90°$, 1.16 MeV (e) 1.16 MeV]

§5-5 Relativistic Dynamics

We recall that there are many instances in which the time rate of doing work is of great importance. This quantity is called the *power*, expressed in units of work divided by units of time—as ergs/sec, in the cgs system of units, or as watts (= joules/sec) in the mks system of units.

The average power is defined as the work done, ΔW, divided by the time interval in which it is done, or

$$\overline{\mathcal{P}} = \frac{\Delta W}{\Delta t}.$$

Applying the definition of work as the scalar product of force and displacement, we have

$$\overline{\mathcal{P}} = \frac{\mathbf{F} \cdot \Delta \mathbf{s}}{\Delta t},$$

which becomes

$$\mathcal{P} = \mathbf{F} \cdot \mathbf{v} \qquad (5\text{-}5.1)$$

in the limit of short times. Thus, the instantaneous power delivered by a force $\mathbf{F}$ to a body moving with velocity $\mathbf{v}$ is the scalar product of the force and the velocity.

We are now able to complete the extension of Newton's second law to rapidly moving systems. In our initial discussion of the second law in Chapter 3, we took the momentum to be a space vector, $\mathbf{p} = m\gamma\mathbf{v}$, with three space components. Later, in §4-6, we saw that momentum and total energy together make up a four-vector whose components are

$$p_1 = p_x = m\gamma v_x, \qquad (5\text{-}5.2a)$$
$$p_2 = p_y = m\gamma v_y, \qquad (5\text{-}5.2b)$$
$$p_3 = p_z = m\gamma v_z, \qquad (5\text{-}5.2c)$$
$$p_4 = E/c^2 = m\gamma. \qquad (5\text{-}5.2d)$$

Following the pattern of Newton's second law, where the space parts of the equations related the force to the time rate of change of the momentum, we ask: What is the time rate of change of the fourth component of the momentum equal to? The time rate of change of energy is power. We therefore infer that the missing fourth component equation from the relativistic form of Newton's second law is that the power is equal to the time rate of change of the energy, in the form

$$\mathcal{P} = \mathbf{F} \cdot \mathbf{v} = \frac{d}{dt} m\gamma c^2. \qquad (5\text{-}5.3)$$

Let us write the four component equations of Newton's second law. We have

$$F_x = \frac{d}{dt} m\gamma v_x, \tag{5-5.4a}$$

$$F_y = \frac{d}{dt} m\gamma v_y, \tag{5-5.4b}$$

$$F_z = \frac{d}{dt} m\gamma v_z, \tag{5-5.4c}$$

$$\mathbf{F} \cdot \mathbf{v} = \frac{d}{dt} m\gamma c^2. \tag{5-5.4d}$$

In Eqs. 5-5.2 a particle of mass m moves with velocity $\mathbf{v}$ with respect to an inertial frame, say the laboratory frame. In this frame $\mathbf{F}$ is the force on the particle and t is the time measured by laboratory observers using their laboratory clocks.

We wish to put Eqs. 5-5.4 in covariant form, in which every quantity is a four-vector, or an invariant quantity which has the same meaning in every inertial frame. First we note that the fourth component of the momentum is not $m\gamma c^2$, but according to Eq. 5-5.2d is $m\gamma$. Therefore we first divide Eq. 5-5.4d by c^2. The next step is to multiply each equation by γ, for reasons that will be made clear soon, to obtain

$$\gamma F_{x,y,z} = \gamma \frac{d}{dt} m\gamma v_{x,y,z}$$

from Eqs. 5-5.4 a-c and

$$\frac{\gamma}{c^2} \mathbf{F} \cdot \mathbf{v} = \gamma \frac{d}{dt} m\gamma,$$

from Eq. 5-5.4d.

We recall that moving clocks run slow by a factor γ (§5-1). If a time interval dt is measured by a laboratory clock, laboratory observers will note that the time interval on a clock moving through the laboratory will be $d\tau$ in the same period, related by the equation

$$dt = \gamma \, d\tau, \tag{5-5.5}$$

which we have seen before, in another notation, as Eq. 2-3.1. The equations take on a simpler form if, instead of measuring time on the laboratory clocks, we measure it on a succession of clocks in different inertial frames, each of which is selected at different points along the path of the particle to be the proper clock for the particle at that instant. The time τ will always be the instantaneous proper time, measured on a clock which is instantaneously at rest with respect to the particle.

Let us substitute for dt into the above equations, from Eq. 5-5.5, to obtain

$$\gamma F_x = \frac{d}{d\tau} m\gamma v_x, \tag{5-5.6a}$$

$$\gamma F_y = \frac{d}{d\tau} m\gamma v_y, \tag{5-5.6b}$$

$$\gamma F_z = \frac{d}{d\tau} m\gamma v_z, \tag{5-5.6c}$$

$$\frac{\gamma}{c^2} \mathbf{F} \cdot \mathbf{v} = \frac{d}{d\tau} m\gamma. \tag{5-5.6d}$$

Equations 5-5.6 differ from Eqs. 5-5.4 only in form, through algebraic manipulation, but there is a significant difference. Every quantity on the right-hand side of the equation is either independent of the inertial frame of the observer, as is $d\tau$, or is a component of a four-vector whose transformation from one frame to another inertial frame is accomplished by the Lorentz transformation equations.

This implies that the quantities on the left-hand side of the equations also are components of a four-vector, which we call the *Minkowski force*, after Hermann Minkowski (1864-1909), who first discovered this formulation of relativistic dynamics. We find it attractive to write Newton's second law in this generalized relativistic form as

$$K_i = \frac{d}{d\tau} p_i, \tag{5-5.7}$$

where K_i is the i'th component of the generalized force whose four components are expressed as

$$K_1 = \gamma F_x, \tag{5-5.8a}$$
$$K_2 = \gamma F_y, \tag{5-5.8b}$$
$$K_3 = \gamma F_z, \tag{5-5.8c}$$

$$K_4 = \frac{\gamma}{c^2}\, \mathbf{F} \cdot \mathbf{v}. \tag{5-5.8d}$$

Equation 5-5.7 is covariant. It has the same form in every inertial frame. Further, the components of K and p measured in one inertial frame are related to the components of K' and p' (the same quantities measured by observers in another inertial frame) by the Lorentz transformation.

The expression of the generalized force now brings the number of relativistic four-vectors we have seen to a total of three. We first saw the Lorentz transformation in connection with the position four-vector whose components were x, y, z, and t. Next we displayed the momentum four-vector, and finally the generalized force four-vector.

In general, it is the attempt of the special theory of relativity to express all physical vector quantities in four-vector form, for in this form we can see clearly how to relate measurements made of these quantities in different inertial frames. This means of expression often displays hitherto unsuspected relatedness, as we saw in connection with the union of momentum and energy in the momentum four-vector. In all cases the components of a four-vector must transform exactly as x, y, z, and t do in the Lorentz transformation.

5-5.1 Show that the application of the Lorentz transformation to the Minkowski force, Eqs. 5-5.8, yields results in agreement with Eqs. 3-3.4.

§5-6 Gravitation and Light We may understand some of the influence of gravitation on light through our studies of the equivalence principle in §3-3 and our studies of the Doppler effect in §5-4. To do so we must extend the results of the Special Theory of Relativity (which deals with observations made on different inertial frames) to observations made on accelerated coordinate frames. We assert that:

1) Acceleration in itself does not affect the rate of a standard

clock or the length of a standard measuring stick, or if it does, the effect may be disregarded in any measurements we are yet able to perform; and

2) Acceleration does not affect the speed of light in vacuum.

We believe these assertions to be reasonable because we would expect that any effect of acceleration would depend on its magnitude. We can always reduce the acceleration to some low value where the assertions would be true.

These assertions amount to the statement that we will regard the Lorentz transformation as instantaneously correct when we use it to compare observations made on an accelerated frame with those made on an inertial frame. Observations of length, time, and the velocity of light made on an inertial frame which is instantaneously at rest with respect to the accelerated frame will agree with similar observations made on the accelerated frame.

Suppose that the accelerated frame is moving in the $+x$ direction with respect to an inertial frame with acceleration a, and that there is a source S at the origin of this frame and a detector D at some coordinate position x in this frame, along its x axis. A pulse of light emitted from the source at $t = 0$ is received by the detector at $t = x/c$ later, at which time the detector is moving at $at = ax/c$ faster than the source was moving when the light was emitted.

Observers located at the detector in the accelerated frame must agree with observers on an inertial frame instantaneously at rest with respect to them about measurements of length and time, and so they must also agree about measurements of frequency. At the instant of detection these observers agree that the source is receding from the detector with speed ax/c, and that the angle between the direction of motion of the source and the detected photon is π. If the proper frequency of the photon is v_0, as measured at the source, observers at the detector must find the frequency Doppler shifted to the red to some new value v.

In the notation of Eqs. 5-4.3 and 5-4.4, the angle $\theta = \pi = \theta'$, the proper frequency of the photon is $v_0 = v'$, and the detected frequency is v. Note that the speed of the proper frame with respect to the laboratory frame is $V = ax/c$ and that $\gamma_0^{-2} = 1 - V^2/c^2$. Then according to Eq. 5-4.3c we have

$$\nu = \nu_0 \gamma_0 (1 - V/c)$$

$$= \nu_0 \frac{(1 - V/c)}{(1 - V^2/c^2)^{1/2}}$$

$$= \nu_0 \left[\frac{1 - V/c}{1 + V/c} \right]^{1/2}$$

$$= \nu_0 (1 - 2V/c + \ldots)^{1/2}$$

$$= \nu_0 (1 - V/c + \ldots)$$

$$\nu = \nu_0 (1 - ax/c^2 + \ldots). \tag{5-6.1}$$

Thus in an accelerated coordinate frame, light moving in the direction of the acceleration will be shifted to the red. By the same argument light moving opposite to the direction of the acceleration will be shifted to the blue.

By the equivalence principle, an accelerated frame is equivalent to a uniform gravitational field. Thus Eq. 5-6.1 is applicable to the case where there is a source at the origin and a detector at x, on an inertial frame in a uniform gravitational field of magnitude $g = a$, but directed in the $-x$ direction. When a light source which emits photons of frequency ν_0 is placed at the bottom of a mine shaft, it will be measured, at the top of the shaft, to have emitted light of frequency ν, given by

$$\nu = \nu_0 (1 - gx/c^2). \tag{5-6.2}$$

This result, which is known as the *gravitational red shift,* has been observed in sunlight and in a shaft 22 meters high by means of a very sharp source of radiation and a correspondingly sharp spectrometer. The observation was made by Pound and Rebka [Phys. Rev. Letters 3, 439 (1959)] by exploiting the recoilless emission and absorption of nuclear γ rays, in the *Mossbauer effect,* discovered in 1958.

As noted from the top of a mine shaft, vibrating atoms at the bottom of the shaft vibrate more slowly (glow redder) than vibrating atoms at the top. Observers at the top of a shaft must note that clocks at the bottom run slow. Since this is a relativistic phenomenon and has nothing to do with the construction of a particular atom or clock, we must conclude that all clocks deep in a mine shaft run more slowly than clocks at the top of the shaft. This observation includes biological clocks as well as other kinds.

While the gravitational red shift may be regarded as being well substantiated experimentally, a second gravitational effect on light, the deflection of a ray of light in a gravitational field, has not yet been fully confirmed quantitatively. Nevertheless, it is instructive to examine the behavior of a light ray in a uniform gravitational field by application of the equivalence principle and aberration. Once again we proceed by studying the accelerated coordinate frame.

We wish first to study the path of a ray of light in an accelerated frame (the unprimed frame) which moves with acceleration a and instantaneous velocity V in the $+x$ direction with respect to an inertial frame (the primed frame) in which the source was at rest at the instant the light was emitted. Equivalently, we may say that the primed frame moves with respect to the unprimed frame with speed $-V$ at the time t when we examine the motion of the light. By Eq. 5-4.4, the light will be seen to move in two different directions in the two frames, as given by

$$\cos \theta = \frac{\cos \theta' - V/c}{1 - \frac{V}{c} \cos \theta'}. \tag{5-6.3}$$

A ray of light directed along the y' axis of the inertial frame continues to move in that direction with velocity c, and the angle θ' is always $\pi/2$. But this is not the case in the accelerated frame, for as the frame moves with increasing speed with respect to the inertial frame, the angle θ which the ray makes with the x axis of the accelerated frame is given by

$$\cos \theta = -V/c, \tag{5-6.4}$$

and since

$$V = at,$$

we find that

$$\cos \theta = -at/c. \qquad (5\text{-}6.5)$$

(Since the aberration effect is of first order in V/c, and any effects of time dilation are of second order in V/c, we need not concern ourselves with any differences between time measured in the accelerated frame and time measured in the inertial frame.)

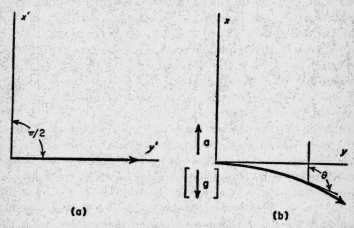

(a)   **(b)**

FIG. 5-6.1   (a) The path of a ray of light in an inertial frame is a straight line in field free space. Here the primed frame is the frame in which the source was instantaneously at rest at the instant the light was emitted. (b) The path of the ray of light observed in the accelerated frame (unprimed) is curved, deflected from the y axis in a direction opposite to the acceleration. (On an inertial frame in a uniform gravitational field the light is deflected in the direction of the field.)

Even though the velocity of light in the accelerated frame is a constant, c, nevertheless the path of a ray of light is not a straight line, but is curved, as in Fig. 5-6.1. To find the path of the ray we note that

$$\sin \theta = (1 - V^2/c^2)^{1/2}, \text{ and}$$

$$\tan \theta = \frac{(1 - V^2/c^2)^{1/2}}{-V/c} = -(c^2/V^2 - 1)^{1/2} = -(c^2/a^2t^2 - 1)^{1/2}.$$

Thus the slope of the light ray is negative.

Since the speed of light is c, the x component of its velocity is

$$c_x = c \cos \theta = -V,$$

and the y component is

$$c_y = c \sin \theta = c(1 - V^2/c^2)^{1/2} = c(1 - a^2t^2/c^2)^{1/2}.$$

Then

$$c_y \cong c \left(1 - \frac{1}{2} \frac{a^2t^2}{c^2}\right).$$

The path of the light ray may be described through the equations

$$x = \int c_x \, dt = -\int V \, dt = -\int at \, dt = -\tfrac{1}{2}at^2 \qquad (5\text{-}6.6a)$$

and

$$y = \int c(1 - a^2t^2/2c^2) \, dt \cong ct \qquad (5\text{-}6.6b)$$

for small a, or where at is much less than c.

To the degree of approximation shown, the light ray follows a parabolic path, as observed in the accelerated (unprimed) frame.

By the equivalence principle the behavior of the light ray in the accelerated frame is equivalent to the behavior of the ray in an inertial frame placed in a uniform gravitational field. Thus, in first approximation, a ray of light emitted in a uniform gravitational field in a direction perpendicular to the field follows the same path we would expect nonrelativistically for a ball projected with velocity c horizontally in a vertical gravitational field.

A ray of light which follows a straight-line path in field free space will be deflected in the direction of the gravitational field intensity when the ray of light is observed from an inertial frame in a uniform gravitational field. The deflection of the path is through the aberration phenomenon, but the result obtained is as if the photon experienced free fall.

CHAPTER BIBLIOGRAPHY

A. A. Bartlett, "Compton Effect," Am. J. Phys. 32, 120 (1964).

A. J. F. Boyle and H. E. Hall, "The Mossbauer Effect," Progress in Physics 25, 442 (1962).

A. H. Compton, "The Scattering of X-rays as Particles," Am. J. Phys. 29, 817 (1961).

K. W. Ford, *The World of Elementary Particles,* Blaisdell Publishing Co., New York, 1963.

D. H. Frisch and A. M. Thorndike, *Elementary Particles,* Momentum Book 1, D. Van Nostrand Company, Inc., Princeton, N.J., 1964.

H. Lustig, "The Mossbauer Effect," Am. J. Phys. 29, 1 (1961).

6 Relativity and Electromagnetism

§6-1 Introduction The original structure of the Faraday-Maxwell theory of electricity and magnetism was built on experimental observation based on the use of charged test bodies as the probe for examining the electric field, and the compass needle as the probe for examining the magnetic field. As an example, the magnetic effect of current was discovered by Oersted through the deflection of a compass needle on initiation of current flow in a nearby wire. In the present discussion* we will retain that structure, and will imagine that we have at our disposal magnetic poles, and currents of magnetic poles through which we may generate fields or probe fields. By this means we expose the fundamental conceptual structure and symmetry of electricity and magnetism, and can develop its inherent relativity. Nevertheless, we must understand that magnetic effects are generally regarded as produced only by moving charges, since no free magnetic pole has been discovered.

The mathematical formulation is most conveniently expressed if we use the vector product, or cross product, notation. The *vector product* **C** of two vectors, **A** and **B**, is itself a vector normal to the plane of **A** and **B**. The sense of **C** is given by a right-hand

---

* The basic outline of the treatment developed here has been published in the American Journal of Physics, Vol. 30, pp. 41-44 (1962), as "The Magnetic Pole in the Formulation of Electricity and Magnetism" by Robert Katz. Some of the material has been developed in fuller detail in an introductory text entitled *Physics* by H. Semat and R. Katz, Holt, Rinehart and Winston (1958). See also "Magnetic Monopoles" by K. W. Ford, Scientific American **209**, 122 (1963).

screw rule. If a right-handed screw is rotated in the sense which rotates vector **A** into the direction of vector **B** when these are drawn from a common origin, the point of the screw advances in the direction of vector **C**, as in Fig. 6-1.1. The magnitude of **C**

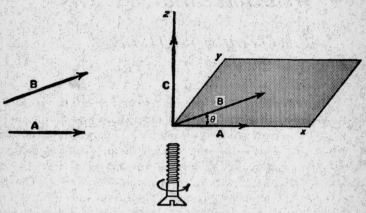

FIG. 6-1.1   The vector product, or cross product, of two vectors A and B is the vector C, written as A × B = C. The magnitude of C is given by C = AB sin θ, and the direction of C is perpendicular to the plane formed by A and B pointing in the direction of advance of a right-hand screw turned so as to advance from A to B. The angle θ is the angle between A and B when these are drawn from a common origin.

is equal to the product of the magnitudes of the two vectors **A** and **B** and the sine of the angle between them (when they are drawn from a common origin). Thus

$$C = AB \sin \theta. \tag{6-1.1}$$

The order of the factors in the vector product is of some importance. While the magnitude of **A × B** is the same as the magnitude of **B × A**, the two vectors are oppositely directed, so that

$$\mathbf{A} \times \mathbf{B} = -\mathbf{B} \times \mathbf{A}. \tag{6-1.2}$$

The vector product **C** is perpendicular to each of the two vectors

A and **B** separately, for it is perpendicular to their common plane.

We have already noted the principle of *conservation of charge,* which states that the total charge content of the universe is constant: charge is neither created nor destroyed. We extend this concept to assert that the charge of a charged body is the same for every inertial observer. In a similar way the theory of electricity and magnetism is structured on the concept of conservation of magnetic poles. We will assume that the pole strength of a magnetic pole is the same for all observers in all inertial frames, without regard to the speed with which it is moving.

§6-2 The Lorentz Force Let us write the Lorentz force on a charged particle as

$$\mathbf{F} = q(\mathbf{E} + \mathbf{v} \times \mathbf{B}) \tag{6-2.1a}$$

and the Lorentz force on a magnetic pole as

$$\mathbf{F} = q_m(\mathbf{H} - \mathbf{v} \times \mathbf{D}). \tag{6-2.1b}$$

These equations are written in the mks system of units. The force **F** is in newtons. The electric charge q is in coulombs. The magnetic pole strength q_m is in webers. The field quantities are point functions in a particular inertial frame; that is, they depend on the choice of the inertial frame in which they are measured as well as on the point in space at which they are measured. This is clear because we have to distinguish between rest and motion of the probe charge or probe pole in determining the field vectors **E, B, H,** and **D.**

The electric field intensity **E,** at a particular point in space and with respect to a particular inertial frame, is the force per unit charge on a positive probe charge at rest in that frame, and is expressed in units of newtons/coulomb. The magnetic field intensity **H,** at a particular point in space and with respect to a particular inertial frame, is the force per unit pole on a north probe pole at rest in that frame, and is expressed in units of newtons/weber. The magnetic flux density **B** is expressed in webers/m² and the electric flux density (electric displacement) **D** is expressed in coulombs/m². The flux densities **B** and **D** may be determined by observing the force on moving probe particles of appropriate character. A moving charge will permit the determination of **B**, while a moving pole will permit the determination of **D**.

The meaning of the field vectors remains the same in vacuum or in a material medium, as described above. The probe charge or probe pole is intended to be of small charge or pole strength so as not to alter the system it probes when it is used to measure the field. In a medium, the fields vary rapidly in the vicinity of atoms. When we wish to determine the rapid variations in the field, we imagine that we probe with a physically small probe, and refer to the field so determined as the *microscopic field*. When we are interested in average properties of the field and do not wish to experience the violent fluctuations as we pass into volumes occupied by individual atoms, we imagine that the probe is physically large and ghost-like so that it can encompass tens or hundreds of atoms at one instant. The field experienced by the large ghost-like probe is called the *macroscopic field*. Regardless of whether we are interested in the macroscopic or microscopic fields, the sense of what we mean by the field quantities remains the same, and is appropriate to the Lorentz force equations.

6-2.1 An airplane making magnetic surveys carries a field-measuring device on a long cable. The earth's magnetic field H is measured to have a horizontal component of 0.18 Øersted. (1 $N/Wb = 4\pi \times 10^{-3}$ Øersted). If the airplane flies at 600 mph through a thunderhead where the vertical component of the electric field E is 3×10^5 N/C, what is the maximum percentage error in the measured magnetic field due to the passage of the magnetometer through the electric field? For purposes of calculation assume that the field is measured by determining the force on the magnetic pole of a compass needle. [0.005 percent]

§6-3 Magnetization and Polarization It is customary to ascribe the effect of a medium on the field to its polarization **P** or its magnetization **M**, the electric or the magnetic dipole moment per unit volume.

An electric dipole consists of a pair of equal positive and negative charges separated by a distance s. If the displacement vector *from negative to positive* charge is s, the electric dipole moment p of the charge pair is

$$p = qs. \tag{6-3.1}$$

When such an electric dipole is placed in a uniform electric field, the net force on the dipole is zero, but the torque on it is

$$G = p \times E. \tag{6-3.2}$$

A magnetic dipole may be imagined to be a pair of equal north (+) and south (−) poles, separated by a distance s. If the displacement vector from south to north pole is s, the magnetic dipole moment of the pair is

$$m = q_m s. \tag{6-3.3}$$

When such a magentic dipole is placed in a uniform magnetic field, the net force on the dipole is zero, but the torque on it is

$$G = m \times H. \tag{6-3.4}$$

Conversely, if a particle or a bit of matter experiences a torque when it is placed in an electric field, we say that it has a net electric dipole moment; and if it experiences a torque when placed in a magnetic field, we say that it has a net magnetic moment. We may conceive of an experiment by which the torque on a bit of uniformly polarized material of volume $\Delta\tau$ placed in a magnetic field is determined, and is analyzed to yield a measure of the polarization through the equation

$$G = (P \, \Delta\tau) \times E. \tag{6-3.5}$$

Similarly, the magnetization of a bit of matter may be found through an analogous experiment and the equation

$$G = (M \, \Delta\tau) \times H. \tag{6-3.6}$$

The polarization is measured in units of electric dipole moment per unit volume, or coulombs/m², while the magnetization is measured in magnetic dipole moment per unit volume, or webers/m².

In introductory texts in physics it is shown that the several electric vectors are related through the equation

$$\mathbf{D} = \epsilon_0\mathbf{E} + \mathbf{P}, \tag{6-3.7a}$$

and that the several magnetic vectors are related through the equation*

$$\mathbf{B} = \mu_0\mathbf{H} + \mathbf{M}. \tag{6-3.7b}$$

The quantity ϵ_0 is called the permittivity of free space, and has the value

$$\epsilon_0 = 8.85 \times 10^{-12} \text{ C}^2/\text{N-m}^2 = (36\pi \times 10^9)^{-1} \text{ C}^2/\text{N-m}^2.$$

The quantity μ_0 is called the permeability of free space, and has the value

$$\mu_0 = 4\pi \times 10^{-7} \text{ Wb}^2/\text{N-m}^2.$$

The product $\epsilon_0\mu_0$ is the reciprocal of the square of the velocity of light in vacuum; that is,

$$\epsilon_0\mu_0 = c^{-2} = (3 \times 10^8 \text{ m/sec})^{-2}.$$

Since vacuum contains neither electric nor magnetic dipoles, the polarization and magnetization of vacuum are zero, and Eqs. 6-3.7 reduce to

$$\mathbf{D} = \epsilon_0\mathbf{E} \tag{6-3.8a}$$

and
$$\mathbf{B} = \mu_0\mathbf{H}. \tag{6-3.8b}$$

§6-4 Transformations of Fields and Flux Densities We call on a result from relativistic mechanics which we have already derived in Eq. 3-4.4. If a force $\mathbf{F}$ acts on a particle in the laboratory frame in which it moves with velocity $\mathbf{v}$, observers on the proper frame of the particle will measure the force on the particle to have a different value, $\mathbf{F}'$. The components of these forces parallel and perpendicular to the velocity $\mathbf{v}$ are given by

$$\mathbf{F}_{||} = \mathbf{F}'_{||} \tag{6-4.1a}$$

and
$$\gamma\mathbf{F}_{\perp} = \mathbf{F}'_{\perp}, \tag{6-4.1b}$$

where $\gamma^{-2} = 1 - v^2/c^2$.

* Some writers prefer an asymmetric treatment in which Eq. 6-3.4 is written as $\mathbf{G} = m \times \mu_0\mathbf{H}$ and Eq. 6-3.7b is written as $\mathbf{B} = \mu_0\mathbf{H} + \mu_0\mathcal{M}$. These differences may be reconciled by setting $\mathbf{m} = \mu_0 m$ and $\mathbf{M} = \mu_0\mathcal{M}$.

To apply Eqs. 6-4.1 to the electromagnetic field and flux density vectors we imagine that we probe the fields at a particular point in space by means of a probe particle, first electric and then magnetic. We shall determine the fields in the laboratory frame and in the proper frame by application of the Lorentz force equations in each frame, and shall relate our determinations through the force transformation equations.

Laboratory observers find the force on the charge q moving with velocity v with respect to the laboratory frame to be

$$\mathbf{F} = q(\mathbf{E} + \mathbf{v} \times \mathbf{B}), \tag{6-4.2a}$$

with component equations taken parallel and perpendicular to the velocity as

$$\mathbf{F}_{||} = q\mathbf{E}_{||} \tag{6-4.2b}$$

and
$$\mathbf{F}_{\perp} = q(\mathbf{E}_{\perp} + \mathbf{v} \times \mathbf{B}). \tag{6-4.2c}$$

Proper observers who are at rest with respect to the charge know that there can be no force on the charge due to a magnetic flux density in their frame, because the charge is at rest. According to these observers the force on the charge must be entirely due to an electric field $\mathbf{E}'$, from the equation

$$\mathbf{F}' = q\mathbf{E}', \tag{6-4.3a}$$

with component equations

$$\mathbf{F}'_{||} = q\mathbf{E}'_{||} \tag{6-4.3b}$$

and
$$\mathbf{F}'_{\perp} = q\mathbf{E}'_{\perp}. \tag{6-4.3c}$$

By means of Eqs. 6-4.1, the dictionary through which forces in the two inertial frames are related, we find that

$$\mathbf{E}'_{||} = \mathbf{E}_{||} \quad \text{and} \quad \mathbf{E}'_{\perp} = \gamma(\mathbf{E}_{\perp} + \mathbf{v} \times \mathbf{B}). \tag{6-4.4a}$$

If we multiply both sides of each of the equations of 6-4.4a by ϵ_0 and apply Eq. 6-3.8, which relates $\mathbf{D}$ to $\mathbf{E}$ and $\mathbf{B}$ to $\mathbf{H}$, we find

$$\mathbf{D}'_{||} = \mathbf{D}_{||} \quad \text{and} \quad \mathbf{D}'_{\perp} = \gamma(\mathbf{D}_{\perp} + \epsilon_0\mu_0\mathbf{v} \times \mathbf{H}). \tag{6-4.4b}$$

With the assumption of the Lorentz force on a moving pole, a parallel argument leads to the transformation equations for $\mathbf{H}$ and $\mathbf{B}$. We obtain

$$\mathbf{H'}_{\parallel} = \mathbf{H}_{\parallel} \quad \text{and} \quad \mathbf{H'}_{\perp} = \gamma(\mathbf{H}_{\perp} - \mathbf{v} \times \mathbf{D}), \qquad (6\text{-}4.4c)$$

$$\mathbf{B'}_{\parallel} = \mathbf{B}_{\parallel} \quad \text{and} \quad \mathbf{B'}_{\perp} = \gamma(\mathbf{B}_{\perp} - \epsilon_0\mu_0\mathbf{v} \times \mathbf{E}). \qquad (6\text{-}4.4d)$$

Equations 6-4.4b and 6-4.4d were derived from 6-4.4a and 6-4.4c for the vacuum case. But in any inertial frame the meaning of the fields and flux densities is the same whether in vacuum or in the medium. The transformation equations remain correct whether the fields and flux densities are measured in vacuum or in a medium. We will see later in §6-7 that these transformation equations may be applied to Eqs. 6-3.7 to yield transformation equations for magnetization and polarization.

Since we may regard either frame as the proper frame in which the probe charge and pole may be placed at rest, we may readily derive the inverse transformations by interchanging the prime and unprime superscripts and replacing $\mathbf{v}$ by $-\mathbf{v}$. We then have

$$\mathbf{E}_{\parallel} = \mathbf{E'}_{\parallel}, \qquad \mathbf{E}_{\perp} = \gamma(\mathbf{E'}_{\perp} - \mathbf{v} \times \mathbf{B'}); \qquad (6\text{-}4.5a)$$

$$\mathbf{D}_{\parallel} = \mathbf{D'}_{\parallel}, \qquad \mathbf{D}_{\perp} = \gamma(\mathbf{D'}_{\perp} - \epsilon_0\mu_0\mathbf{v} \times \mathbf{H'}); \qquad (6\text{-}4.5b)$$

$$\mathbf{H}_{\parallel} = \mathbf{H'}_{\parallel}, \qquad \mathbf{H}_{\perp} = \gamma(\mathbf{H'}_{\perp} + \mathbf{v} \times \mathbf{D'}); \qquad (6\text{-}4.5c)$$

$$\mathbf{B}_{\parallel} = \mathbf{B'}_{\parallel}, \qquad \mathbf{B}_{\perp} = \gamma(\mathbf{B'}_{\perp} + \epsilon_0\mu_0\mathbf{v} \times \mathbf{E'}). \qquad (6\text{-}4.5d)$$

The transformation equations 6-4.4 and 6-4.5 relate the fields and flux densities in the laboratory (unprimed) frame and in a second frame (the primed frame) which is moving with velocity $\mathbf{v}$ with respect to the laboratory frame.

These equations provide the basis for vague statements which are sometimes encountered, such as "motion with respect to an electric field makes a magnetic field" or "A moving magnetic field makes an electric field."

6-4.1 In the $n = 1$ Bohr orbit of hydrogen $(r = 0.529\text{A}°)$ find the electric flux density at the position of the electron (a) in the laboratory frame (D) and (b) in the proper frame of the electron (D'). Find the magnetic field intensity at the position of the electron (c) in the laboratory frame (H), and (d) in the proper frame (H') of the electron. The speed of motion of the electron may be obtained from the quantum condition on angular momentum $mvr = h/2\pi$. [(a) 0.72×10^{-18} C/m² (b) 0.72×10^{-18} C/m² (c) 0 (d) 1.6×10^{-12} N/Wb)]

§6-5 Electromagnetic Induction
There are two aspects to electromagnetic induction, as reflected in the transformer and in

the generator (dynamo). A changing flux through a loop of wire generates the electromotive force of the transformer. While this effect may be conceived as the electric field due to a displacement current of magnetic poles (following §6-6), we shall devote no space to its exposition. The generator effect is due to the motion of the wires of the generator with respect to a static magnetic field, and is best understood in relativistic terms as due to the transformation of electromagnetic fields and flux densities.

Suppose a wire moves through a magnetic field of flux density **B**. In the frame of the laboratory the electric field intensity is zero, but in the frame of the wire the electric field intensity **E′** given by Eq. 6-4.4a is

$$\mathbf{E'} = \gamma \mathbf{v} \times \mathbf{B}. \tag{6-5.1}$$

If a wire of length s slides over a fixed conductor a consisting of two parallel tracks which are electrically connected at one end, through a magnetic field in the laboratory frame, as in Fig. 6-5.1, current flows in the circuit. The *electromotive force* ε induced in this process is the work done in carrying a unit positive probe charge around a closed loop which is partly at rest in the laboratory frame, and partly at rest in the moving frame, for the loop is made up of the fixed conductor a and the moving conductor s. Integrating around the loop, we have

$$\varepsilon = \oint \mathbf{E} \cdot d\mathbf{s} = \int_a \mathbf{E} \cdot d\mathbf{s} + \int_s \mathbf{E'} \cdot d\mathbf{s} = \int_s \gamma \mathbf{v} \times \mathbf{B} \cdot d\mathbf{s}. \tag{6-5.2}$$

It is customary to ignore the factor γ in introductory treatments, for the velocity is assumed small compared to c, and to evaluate the integral as

$$\varepsilon = \gamma Bsv \cong Bsv \tag{6-5.3}$$

in the geometry of Fig. 6-5.1.

Since the motion of a wire through a uniform magnetic field is the prototype for the design of electric generators, we see that the commercial generation of electric power depends on the inherent relativistic character of electricity and magnetism.

The effect of the motion of the wire through the field has sometimes been attributed to "flux cutting." It is difficult to conceive of the Faraday disk or its linear counterpart, the conducting bar moving along its length in a magnetic field, in flux-cutting terms. The Faraday disk is shown in Fig. 6-5.2a, and its linear counterpart in Fig. 6-5.2b. These devices are sometimes classed as *homopolar generators*.

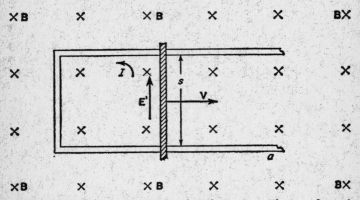

FIG. 6-5.1 A current *I* flows in a closed circuit made up of a wire *s* which slides over parallel tracks through a region of flux density B (measured in the frame in which the tracks are at rest). An electromotive force is induced in the circuit. The wire is sometimes called the "seat of emf," for the only contribution to the emf is in that portion of the circuit containing the moving wire. Of course, the wire does not slide by itself. An outside agency must exert a force in the direction of v to keep the wire sliding with constant speed, and to provide the mechanical energy which is converted to electrical energy.

As in section §5-6, we will assert that acceleration does not affect the validity of the Lorentz transformations and their consequences. We will treat both cases illustrated in Fig. 6-5.2 in the same manner. The magnetic flux density has been determined to be **B** and the electric field to be zero in the laboratory frame. At a point P fixed to the moving conductor, we have, by Eq. 6-4.4a, that the electric field **E′** is given by

$$\mathbf{E'} = \gamma \mathbf{v} \times \mathbf{B}. \tag{6-5.1}$$

Thus, if the bar in Fig. 6-5.2b is of width l, the potential differ-ence (emf) across the edges of the bar is given by

$$\mathcal{E} = \gamma v B l. \qquad (6\text{-}5.4)$$

In the case of the disk, the instantaneous proper frame of a

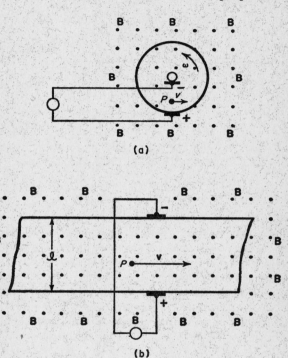

(a)

(b)

FIG. 6-5.2 (a) Faraday disk generator. A copper disk rotating in a uni-form field generates a potential difference between brushes on the axle and the rim. (b) Linear counterpart of the Faraday disk. A long bar moves through a uniform magnetic field.

point P which is r distant from the center is moving with speed $v = \omega r$ with respect to the laboratory frame. The electric field is directed radially outward. Concentric cylinders centered on the axle are equipotential surfaces. The electric field has magnitude

$$E' = \gamma \omega r B \qquad (6\text{-}5.5)$$

and the potential difference (emf) is

$$\mathcal{E} = \int \omega Br \, dr = \omega Br^2/2 \qquad (6\text{-}5.6)$$

in the limit of low speeds.

6-5.1 A wire of length s moves with velocity $\mathbf{v}$ at right angles to a magnetic field of flux density $\mathbf{B}$, the wire being perpendicular to both $\mathbf{v}$ and $\mathbf{B}$. Find the force on a charge q at rest in the wire, as determined by (a) a laboratory observer and (b) an observer in the frame of the wire. The proper observer (at rest in the frame of the wire) attributes the force to an electric field $\mathbf{E}$. (c) Give the value of this electric field. (d) What is the value of the emf across the ends of this wire as determined by the proper observer? [(a) $q\mathbf{v} \times B$ (b) $\gamma q\mathbf{v} \times B$ (c) $\gamma \mathbf{v} \times \mathbf{B}$ (d) γvsB].

6-5.2 A wire 200 cm long is moved in the $+x$ direction at a speed of 50 m/sec. so that the wire is always parallel to the z direction. The magnetic field has components $B_x = 0.4$ Wb/m^2, $B_y = 0.8$ Wb/m^2, $B_z = -0.6$ Wb/m^2. Find the emf induced in the wire. [80 volts, in the $+z$ direction]

§6-6 Field of a Moving Charge At low speed a charged body generates an electric flux density $\mathbf{D}$ and a magnetic field intensity $\mathbf{H}$ given by

$$\mathbf{D} = \frac{q\mathbf{1}_r}{4\pi r^2} \qquad (6\text{-}6.1a)$$

and

$$\mathbf{H} = \mathbf{v} \times \mathbf{D} = \frac{q\mathbf{v} \times \mathbf{1}_r}{4\pi r^2}. \qquad (6\text{-}6.1b)$$

Equation 6-6.1b is equivalent to the Biot-Savart law for the magnetic field due to a current element, as we may see by replacing $q\mathbf{v}$ by $i \, d\mathbf{l}$.

Similarly, a slowly moving magnetic pole generates a magnetic flux density $\mathbf{B}$ and an electric field intensity $\mathbf{E}$ given by

$$\mathbf{B} = \frac{q_m\mathbf{1}_r}{4\pi r^2} \qquad (6\text{-}6.1c)$$

and

$$\mathbf{E} = -\mathbf{v} \times \mathbf{B} = -\frac{q_m\mathbf{v} \times \mathbf{1}_r}{4\pi r^2}. \qquad (6\text{-}6.1d)$$

An equation equivalent to the Biot-Savart law for the electric field due to an element of pole current may be obtained by replacing $q_m \mathbf{v}$ by $i_m\, d\mathbf{l}$.

Equations 6-6.1 are valid in vacuum or in a homogeneous medium, in the reference frame in which the particle velocity is $\mathbf{v}$ and where $\mathbf{1}_r$ is a unit vector directed from the particle to the field point P located r away.

To find the field equations valid at arbitrary speeds we apply the relativistic transformations to the Coulomb field of a charged particle at rest in its proper frame. Let us call the direction of motion of the particle in the laboratory frame the x direction. Then the proper (primed) observer notes the electric flux density to have components

$$D'_x = qx'/4\pi r'^3, \quad D'_y = qy'/4\pi r'^3, \quad D'_z = qz'/4\pi r'^3, \quad (6\text{-}6.2)$$

and the magnetic field to be zero.

An observer in the laboratory (unprimed) frame notes that the particle is moving with velocity $\mathbf{v}$, and applies Eqs. 6-4.5 to translate the proper field components into laboratory field component values. He finds

$$D_x = D'_x, \quad D_y = \gamma D'_y, \quad D_z = \gamma D'_z, \qquad (6\text{-}6.3a)$$
$$H_x = H'_x = 0 = (\mathbf{v} \times \mathbf{D})_x,$$
$$H_y = \gamma(\mathbf{v} \times \mathbf{D}')_y = (\mathbf{v} \times \mathbf{D})_y,$$
$$H_z = \gamma(\mathbf{v} \times \mathbf{D}')_z = (\mathbf{v} \times \mathbf{D})_z,$$

or
$$\mathbf{H} = \mathbf{v} \times \mathbf{D}, \qquad (6\text{-}6.3b)$$

in agreement with the relationship between $\mathbf{H}$ and $\mathbf{D}$ at low speeds given in Eq. 6-6.1b.

To express the fields in terms of the position of the particle in laboratory coordinates we must take note of the Lorentz contraction. If the charged particle is at the common origin of both frames, a field point whose coordinates in the proper frame are x', y', z' will have laboratory coordinates x, y, z, related through the equations

$$x' = \gamma x, \quad y' = y, \quad z' = z, \qquad (6\text{-}6.4)$$

and the quantity

$$r'^2 = x'^2 + y'^2 + z'^2$$

transforms into

$$s^2 = \gamma^2 x^2 + y^2 + z^2 = \gamma^2 r^2 (1 - \beta^2 \sin^2 \theta).$$

With these results we find from Eq. 6-6.3

$$D_x = \gamma q x / 4\pi s^3, \quad D_y = \gamma q y / 4\pi s^3, \quad D_z = \gamma q z / 4\pi s^3,$$

which may be expressed in terms of r and θ as

$$\mathbf{D} = \frac{q\mathbf{1}_r}{4\pi\gamma^2 r^2 (1 - \beta^2 \sin^2 \theta)^{3/2}} \tag{6-6.5a}$$

and $$\mathbf{H} = \mathbf{v} \times \mathbf{D}. \tag{6-6.5b}$$

The electric field of a rapidly moving charged particle is not spherically symmetric. The fields ahead of the particle ($\theta = 0$) and directly behind it ($\theta = \pi$) are reduced, while the field is increased in the transverse direction, as shown in Fig. 6-6.1.

When a relativistic charged particle passes through matter, an

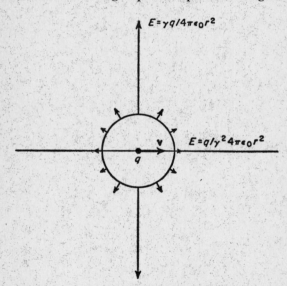

FIG. 6-6.1   Electric field intensities at fixed distance from a rapidly moving charge, determined in the laboratory frame ($\gamma = 10$).

atomic electron experiences a sudden thrust to the side as the charged particle goes by. In the limit $\beta \to 0$ and $\gamma \to 1$ we find that Eqs. 6-6.5 approach the nonrelativistic forms given in Eqs. 6-6.1.

Similar results may be obtained for the fields of a rapidly moving pole.

6-6.1 A proton moves through the laboratory at $\gamma = 10$. What is the electric field intensity E at points 1 millimicron from the proton (a) ahead, (b) at $30°$, (c) at $60°$, (d) at $90°$ to the proton's motion? [(a) $E_{0°} = 1.4 \times 10^7 \text{N/C}$ (b) $E_{30°} = 1.8\ E_{0°}$ (c) $E_{60°} = 22\ E_{0°}$ (d) $E_{90°} = 1000 E_{0°}$.]

6-6.2 Two electrons move abreast down the axis of a linear accelerator in parallel paths at $\beta = 0.995$ $(\gamma = 10)$, separated transversely by one millimicron. (a) Find the force between them in their proper frame. (b) Find the force between them in the laboratory frame. Do this two ways. First, transform the result of part (a) to the laboratory frame. Next compute the fields in the laboratory frame, and then apply the Lorentz force equations to find the force in the laboratory frame. Note that a smaller force is experienced in the laboratory frame than in the proper frame. In the laboratory beams of rapidly moving particles spread apart more slowly than beams of slowly moving charged particles through this effect, called *relativistic focussing*. [(a) 2.3×10^{-10} N, repulsive (b) 2.3×10^{-11} N, repulsive]

6-6.3 Prepare polar plots of E (at 1 mμ) vs. θ for electrons whose laboratory energy is (a) mc^2 (b) $10\ mc^2$ (c) $100\ mc^2$. Plot $E(\theta)$ as the radial distance from the origin at different angles θ with the direction of motion in the laboratory frame.

§6-7 Tranformation of Polarization and Magnetization We may find transformation equations for magnetization and polarization by applying Eqs. 6-3.7, which relate the field and flux density to the properties of the medium, to the transformation equations for **E, B, D,** and **H** which we have already derived.

We find

$$\mathbf{D}'_{\perp} = \gamma(\mathbf{D}_{\perp} + \epsilon_0 \mu_0 \mathbf{v} \times \mathbf{H}).$$

Now

$$\mathbf{D}'_{\perp} = \epsilon_0 \mathbf{E}'_{\perp} + \mathbf{P}'_{\perp}$$

and

$$\mathbf{D}_{\perp} = \epsilon_0 \mathbf{E}_{\perp} + \mathbf{P}_{\perp},$$

and

$$\mathbf{E}'_{\perp} = \gamma(\mathbf{E}_{\perp} + \mathbf{v} \times \mathbf{B})$$

so that

$$\epsilon_0\gamma(\mathbf{E}_{\perp} + \mathbf{v} \times \mathbf{B}) + \mathbf{P}'_{\perp} = \gamma(\epsilon_0\mathbf{E}_{\perp} + \mathbf{P}_{\perp} + \epsilon_0\mu_0\mathbf{v} \times \mathbf{H}).$$

Thus

$$\mathbf{P}'_{\perp} = \gamma(\mathbf{P}_{\perp} - \epsilon_0\mathbf{v} \times (\mathbf{B} - \mu_0\mathbf{H}),$$

or

$$\mathbf{P}'_{\perp} = \gamma(\mathbf{P}_{\perp} - \epsilon_0\mathbf{v} \times \mathbf{M}). \tag{6-7.1a}$$

Similarly

$$\mathbf{P}'_{||} = \mathbf{P}_{||}, \tag{6-7.1b}$$
$$\mathbf{M}'_{\perp} = \gamma(\mathbf{M}_{\perp} + \mu_0\mathbf{v} \times \mathbf{P}), \tag{6-7.1c}$$
$$\mathbf{M}'_{||} = \mathbf{M}_{||}. \tag{6-7.1d}$$

In the usual way, the inverse transformation is obtained by interchanging prime and unprime superscripts and by replacing **v** by −**v**. We have

$$\mathbf{P}_{\perp} = \gamma(\mathbf{P}'_{\perp} + \epsilon_0\mathbf{v} \times \mathbf{M}'), \tag{6-7.2a}$$
$$\mathbf{P}_{||} = \mathbf{P}'_{||}, \tag{6-7.2b}$$
$$\mathbf{M}_{\perp} = \gamma(\mathbf{M}'_{\perp} - \mu_0\mathbf{v} \times \mathbf{P}'), \tag{6-7.2c}$$
$$\mathbf{M}_{||} = \mathbf{M}'_{||}. \tag{6-7.2d}$$

Thus a moving electret which has only permanent polarization in its proper frame may appear to laboratory observers to be magnetized. A moving magnet appears to be polarized.

We may readily interpret these results in elementary terms if we note that the magnetic moment of a current loop is given by

$$m = \mu_0 iA, \tag{6-7.3a}$$

and the electric dipole moment of a pole current loop is given by

$$p = \epsilon_0 i_m A, \tag{6-7.3b}$$

where A is the area of the loop. The direction of the moment is given by a right-hand rule for Eq. 6-7.3a and a left-hand rule for Eq. 6-7.3b. The magnetic moment of a current loop may be derived by calculating the torque on a loop of current in a uniform magnetic field. We recall that the magnetic force on a current element may be obtained from the Lorentz force on a moving charge by replacing qv by $i\,dl$. The magnetic moment may then be obtained by comparison of this result with Eq. 6-3.4 for the torque on a magnetic dipole. The electric dipole moment of a pole current loop may be obtained through use of an analogus recipe, with $i_m dl$ replacing $q_m v$ in the Lorentz force equation, and the result of the torque calculation compared to Eq. 6-3.2.

Let us now examine a moving ribbon of polarized material of proper polarization $\mathbf{P}'$ (a ribbon electret), moving parallel to its length and polarized perpendicular to its direction of motion, as shown in Fig. 6-7.1a.

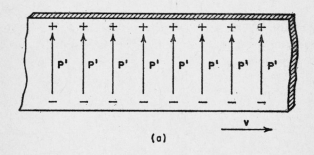

(a)

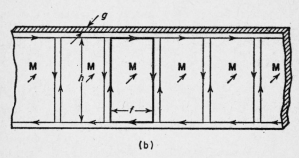

(b)

FIG. 6-7.1

In the laboratory frame, from Eq. 6-7.2 we find

$$\mathbf{P} = \gamma \mathbf{P}' \qquad \text{(6-7.4a)}$$

and

$$\mathbf{M} = -\gamma \mu_0 \mathbf{v} \times \mathbf{P}'. \qquad \text{(6-7.4b)}$$

The ribbon appears to be differently polarized in the laboratory frame, and magnetized as well. Note that the difference in polarization vanishes in the limit $\gamma \to 1$, but that the magnetization remains, for this is a first-order effect.

These results may be easily understood from elementary considerations. A polarized ribbon may be thought of as a collection of large dipoles, whose negative charges are all along the bottom edge of the ribbon and whose positive charges are at the top edge. The motion of positive charge to the right constitutes a flow of current to the right, but the motion of negative charges to the right constitutes a flow of current to the left. We may therefore imagine the ribbon to be replaced by two currents. For purposes of calculation we add pairs of opposing currents crossing from the top edge of the ribbon to the bottom edge, and now conceive of replacing the moving ribbon by a stationary ribbon of current loops, as in Fig. 6-7.1b. By the right-hand rule we note that the magnetization is into the paper.

A ribbon of width h and thickness g contains volume fgh in a length f. The total dipole moment contained in this volume is $Pfgh$. If λ is the edge polarization charge per unit length, then we have

$$\lambda fh = Pfgh,$$

or
$$\lambda = Pg.$$

The current flow is the charge per second flowing past a point in space. If the ribbon moves at speed v, then

$$i = \lambda v = Pgv.$$

The magnetic moment in the section is the product of the magnetization times the volume, and is also given by Eq. 6-7.3a so that

$$Mfgh = \mu_0 Pgvfh,$$

or
$$M = \mu_0 Pv.$$

This result is in agreement with our transformation equation 6-7.4b in the limit of low velocities. Since we would expect the polarization to be the same in both frames, this conclusion from Eq. 6-7.4a is of no surprise.

In precisely the same way we imagine a ribbon of magnetized material to consist of pole currents along the edges of the ribbon, and analyze the problem as one of electric dipole moment arising from pole current loops. A laboratory observer measuring a moving strip of magnetic ribbon finds it polarized as well as magnetized.

§6-8 **The Unipolar Generator** In July 1851, Faraday entered into his diary a discussion of an experiment in which a current was induced in a wire which made sliding contact with points near the axis and the surface of a rotating cylindrical magnet, as shown schematically in Fig. 6-8.1a.

Just as in the case of the Faraday disk we shall examine the generator and its linear counterpart, schematized in Fig. 6-8.1b, at the same time. As before, we shall assert that acceleration does not affect the validity of the Lorentz transformations and their consequences.

We idealize the magnet and ribbon counterpart by asserting that they are so constructed that we may neglect $\mathbf{H}'$ as very small, and that they are uniformly magnetized to a magnetization $\mathbf{M}'$, so that $\mathbf{B}'$ within the magnetized material is also uniform and equal to $\mathbf{M}'$, by Eq. 6-3.7b.

We may therefore consider that in the proper frame of the ribbon there is magnetization $\mathbf{M}'$ and flux density $\mathbf{B}'$. In the laboratory, from Eqs. 6-4.5, the magnetic flux density is

$$\mathbf{B} = \gamma \mathbf{B}' \tag{6-8.1a}$$

and the electric field intensity is

$$\mathbf{E} = -\gamma \mathbf{v} \times \mathbf{B}'. \tag{6-8.1b}$$

Let us briefly revert to the elementary idea that the emf is the open circuit potential difference across the terminals of a source, just as in a battery.

If the thickness of the ribbon is g, then the potential difference (emf) across its face is of magnitude

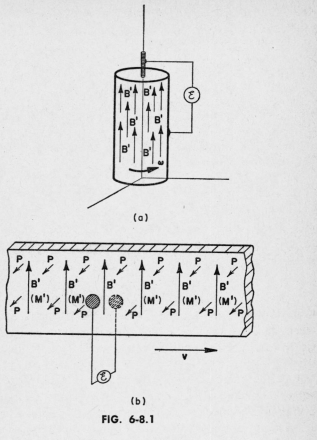

(a)

(b)

FIG. 6-8.1

$$\mathcal{E} = \gamma v B' g \qquad (6\text{-}8.2a)$$

We may analyze the behavior of the ribbon in another way. From Eq. 6-7.2a moving magnetization appears in the laboratory frame as polarization, with

$$\mathcal{P} = \gamma \epsilon_0 \mathbf{v} \times \mathbf{M}'.$$

From electrostatic theory, there is a potential discontinuity across the opposite faces of a dipole layer of dipole moment per unit area $\mathcal{P}$, given by $\mathcal{P}/\epsilon_0$. If the polarization of a ribbon of thickness g is **P**, then its dipole moment per unit area is

$$\mathcal{P} = \mathbf{P}g,$$

so that

$$\mathcal{E} = \gamma v M' g, \tag{6-8.2b}$$

which is the result of Eq. 6-8.2a, if we note that in this case $\mathbf{M'} = \mathbf{B'}$.

The same analysis applies to the rotating magnet of Fig. 6-8.1a. Here $\mathbf{v} = \boldsymbol{\omega} \times \mathbf{r}$, and again as in Eq. 6-8.1b

$$\mathbf{E} = -\gamma(\boldsymbol{\omega} \times \mathbf{r}) \times \mathbf{B'}. \tag{6-8.1b}$$

The electric field is radial. We may drop the vector notation. We note that cylinders concentric with the axis are equipotential surfaces, and that the potential difference between axis and surface is given by

$$\mathcal{E} = \int_0^R \omega r B' \, dr = \omega B' R^2/2, \tag{6-8.3}$$

in the limit of small speeds. The potential difference (emf) between the axis and surface of the cylinder is equal to the flux within the rotating cylinder which would be cut by a radial wire in one second.

§6-9 Postscript   Unlike classical mechanics, classical electromagnetic theory was only clarified, not essentially modified by the special theory of relativity. In fact, relativity theory grew out of electrodynamics, and Einstein's original paper on the subject was entitled "On the Electrodynamics of Moving Bodies." As a result of the complete inner consistency between them, the connections between electromagnetism and relativity may be approached in a variety of ways. One is to follow the historical path of examining the experimental evidence for the incompatibility of electromagnetism and Newtonian mechanics. Through this avenue the relativistic modifications of mechanics which reconcile the difficulties may be found. Such a procedure has been followed in many older texts and treatises on classical electricity and magnetism, which may be found among the references at the end of this chapter.

While the concept of a magnetic pole was used freely in the work of Maxwell, his predecessors, and his followers, the subsequent discovery of the electron and the failure of experimental physics to discover the corresponding particle, the free magnetic pole, has led many physicists to avoid the use of the pole concept in their exposition of electromagnetic theory (see Coulomb's Law Committee report). In this case all field quantities are traced to electric charges and currents. The magnetic effect of currents may then be derived from the Lorentz transformation and Coulomb's law. A full treatment of the transformation of the several electromagnetic field quantities by this procedure may require considerable mathematical sophistication. Whatever expository path is chosen, the destination is the same, for the field transformation equations depend on Maxwell's equations, and not on the manner of their exposition. References have been provided which treat some of these questions by alternate procedures.

CHAPTER BIBLIOGRAPHY

E. Amaldi, G. Baroni, H. Bradner, H. G. deCarvalho, L. Hoffman, A. Manfredini, and G. Vanderhaeghe, *Search for Dirac Magnetic Poles*, CERN 63-13 (1963).

R. Becker and F. Sauter, *Electromagnetic Theory and Relativity*, Blaisdell Publishing Co., New York, 1964.

S. Devons, "*The Search for the Magnetic Monopole,*" Science Progress **51**, 601 (1963).

B. Dibner, *Oersted and the Discovery of Electromagnetism*, Blaisdell Publishing Co., New York, 1962.

R. P. Feynman, R. B. Leighton, and M. Sands, *The Feynman Lectures on Physics*, Addison-Wesley Publishing Co., Inc., Reading, Mass.

F. Gutmann, "The Electret," Rev. Mod. Phys. **20**, 457 (1948).

J. D. Jackson, *Classical Electrodynamics*, John Wiley and Sons, Inc., New York, 1962.

E. C. Kemble, Chairman, Coulomb's Law Committee, "The Teaching of Electricity and Magnetism at the College Level," Am. J. Phys. **18**, 1 and 69 (1950).

J. C. Maxwell, *A Treatise on Electricity and Magnetism* (2 vol.) (reprint), Dover Publications, Inc., New York, 1954.

W. K. H. Panofsky and M. Phillips, *Classical Electricity and Magnetism*, Addison-Wesley Publishing Company, Inc., Reading, Mass., 1955.

E. M. Pugh and E. W. Pugh, *Principles of Electricity and Magnetism*, Addison-Wesley Publishing Company, Inc., Reading, Mass.

W. T. Scott, "Resource Letter FC-1 on the Evolution of the Electromagnetic Field Concept," Am. J. Phys. **31**, 1 (1963).

F. S. Shire, *Classical Electricity and Magnetism*, Cambridge University Press, Cambridge, 1960.

A. Sommerfeld, *Electrodynamics* (*Lectures on Theoretical Physics*, Vol. 3) (reprint), Academic Press, New York (1964).

E. Whittaker, *History of the Theories of Aether and Electricity* (2 vol.) (reprint), Harper Torchbook, New York.

General Bibliography

M. Born, *Einstein's Theory of Relativity* (reprint), Dover Publications, Inc., New York, 1962.

E. U. Condon and H. Odishaw, *Handbook of Physics,* McGraw-Hill Book Company, Inc., New York, 1962.

A. Einstein, H. A. Lorentz, H. Minkowski, and H. Weyl, *The Principle of Relativity* (reprint), Dover Publications, Inc., New York, 1923.

G. Holton, "Resource Letter SRT-1 on Special Relativity Theory," Am. J. Phys. **30**, 462 (1962). Selected reprints of journal articles from this bibliography are available as a reprint book on special relativity theory from the American Institute of Physics, 335 E. 45 St., New York 17, N.Y.

G. Joos, *Theoretical Physics,* Hafner Publishing Co., New York, 1950.

L. Landau and E. Lifshitz, *The Classical Theory of Fields,* Addison-Wesley Publishing Company, Inc., Reading, Mass., rev. 2d ed., 1962.

C. Moller, *The Theory of Relativity,* Oxford University Press, Oxford, 1934.

W. Pauli, *Theory of Relativity,* Pergamon Press, New York, 1958.

H. Semat and R. Katz, *Physics,* Holt, Rinehart and Winston, New York, 1958.

R. S. Shankland, "Conversations with Albert Einstein," Am. J. Phys. **31**, 47 (1963).

Index